Fascinating Fibonaccis
Mystery and Magic
in Numbers

Trudi Hammel Garland

DALE SEYMOUR PUBLICATIONS

Editing: Kathleen Engelberg
Illustrations: Shirley Nootbaar
Cover Design: John Edeen

The author and publisher gratefully acknowledge permission to reprint the following copyrighted material:

Drawing of sneezewort, page 13. Reprinted with permission from H.E. Huntley, *The Divine Proportion* (New York: Dover Publications, 1970), p. 163, figure 12.5.
Floor plan of tomb of Ramses IV, page 25. Reprinted with permission from Matila Ghyka, *The Geometry of Art and Life* (New York: Dover Publications, 1977), plate LVIII.
Mosaic ruler, page 29. Adapted with permission from Richard E.M. Moore, "Mosaic Units: Patterns in Ancient Mosaics," *Fibonacci Quarterly* 8 (April 1970), p. 309.
Diagram of musical movement, page 37. Adapted with permission from Erno Lendavi, *Béla Bartók, An Analysis of His Music* (London: Kahn & Averill, 1971, available in the United States from Humanities Press, Inc., Atlantic Highlands, NJ 07716), pp. 28 (figure 22) and 29 (figure 23).
Four of nature's pentagons, page 17. Reprinted with permission from LeRoy C. Dalton, *Algebra in the Real World* (Palo Alto, CA: Dale Seymour Publications, 1983), pp. 186 and 187.
Four musical staffs, page 39. From *The Schillinger System of Musical Composition* by Joseph Schillinger.

Published by Da Capo Press, Inc. Copyright © 1941, 1942, 1946 by Carl Fischer, Inc., New York. Copyrights renewed. International copyright secured. Used by permission of Carl Fischer, Inc., New York.
Wave diagrams, pages 57-59. Reprinted by permission from Robert Prechter and Alfred J. Frost, *The Elliot Wave Principle* (Gainesville, GA: New Classics Library, 1978), pp. 20 (figure 1), 21 (figure 2), 22 (figure 3), and 94 (figure 73).
Le Corbusier's Modular, page 60. Reprinted with permission from the 1977 *Yearbook of Science and the Future,* copyright © 1976, Encyclopaedia Britannica, Inc., Chicago, Illinois.
Drawings of bones in hand and rectangle in index finger, page 61. Reprinted with permission from Bruce Haughey, *Dynamic Composition* (Haughey Studios, 2324 Spruce, Billings, MT 59101), pp. 26 (diagram 6) and 30 (diagram 8).
Lists of Fibonacci and Lucas numbers and their factorizations, pages 85-88. Reprinted with permission from Brother U. Alfred Brousseau, *An Introduction to Fibonacci Discovery* (San Jose, CA: San Jose State University, The Fibonacci Association, 1965), pp. 52 and 55.
Hindu-Arabic numerals, page 93. Reprinted with permission from D.E. Smith, *History of Mathematics* (New York: Dover Publications, 1923), p. 71.

Printed in the United States of America. Published simultaneously in Canada.

Order number DS01711
ISBN 0-86651-343-4

DALE
SEYMOUR
PUBLICATIONS®

To Bruce
for his encouragement,
good humor,
and love

Contents

Acknowledgments

On the occasion of the 100th anniversary of The Head-Royce School in Oakland, California, I would like to express my appreciation to the following:

The Board of Trustees and the Headmaster, Paul Chapman, for inspiring and encouraging the preparation of this manuscript.

The faculty, for contributing generously of its collective expertise — most especially Steven Gregg, Vera Kerekes, Louise Stevens, and the library staff.

The middle school students, whose insatiable curiosity and spirited enthusiasm helped me focus on the need for a concise, understandable summary of Fibonacci numbers.

Additionally, I feel a sense of gratitude toward numerous friends and acquaintances. Among them are Professor Donald Kaplan of the University of California, Berkeley, and Brother Alfred Brousseau of St. Mary's College for their scholarly assistance; Hertha Hammel and Kathryn Garland for their initial research and editing; Dr. Alan Sampson for sharing his informed opinions; Shirley Nootbaar for her unique vision and cheerful devotion to the project; Beverly Cory for her attention to detail and commitment to quality; and the staff of Dale Seymour Publications for their on-going support.

Preface

For many years I have been captivated and intrigued by Fibonacci numbers. It has been enormously satisfying to share what I know about them with my young teenage students. Their responses have run the gamut from profound disbelief to patronizing good humor, sprinkled with scientific inquisitiveness. Invariably they ask for more information that they might take home to share with family and friends, demonstrating a confidence in others' interest in the subject and thus revealing their own. Unfortunately the information they seek has been deeply buried in scientific journals or aging mathematical literature, occasionally surfacing as one perfunctory page in a textbook or as a scholarly article in a popular periodical.

It seemed to me that the time had come to collect and sort out what is currently known about this fascinating subject, to make it understandable and to excite the curiosity of believers and skeptics alike. What is so special about these numbers? Where did they come from? Why do they keep popping up in unlikely, unrelated places? Where might they be that no one has yet thought to look? What answers might they hold for the world, if not the universe?

T.H.G.

CHAPTER 1

Origins and Definitions

Once upon a time, nearly 800 years ago, there lived a brilliant mathematician named Leonardo of Pisa. Actually, his name was simply Leonardo, but since he was born in the town of Pisa in Italy, where the famous Leaning Tower is located, he was called Leonardo of Pisa. When he began writing books about mathematics, he nicknamed himself "Fibonacci" for writing purposes.* Many authors do this; Mark Twain's real name was Samuel Clemens.

Under the name Fibonacci, Leonardo wrote one particularly well-known work, *Liber Abaci*. This book was very influential in introducing Arabic numerals—the familiar 0, 1, 2, 3, 4, 5, 6, 7, 8, and 9—into Western culture. Leonardo had encountered them in his travels as a young man and considered them superior to Roman numerals, which were widely used in Europe at the time. He could readily see that 48 was easier to deal with than XLVIII.

Liber Abaci (in English, "Book of the Abacus" or "Book of Calculating") also contained interesting story problems, which Leonardo liked to invent. One well-known problem involved speculating

---

*The correct way to pronounce his name is "Fee-buh-NOTCH-ee."

on what would happen if a pair of rabbits were put into a walled enclosure to breed:

How many pairs of rabbits will there be after a year if it is assumed that every month each pair produces one new pair, which begins to bear young two months after its own birth?

The problem can be solved by drawing a picture beginning with the original pair of rabbits in the first month of the year (see figure 1-1).

Figure 1-1   JAN. 1

By the second month, they will have produced a pair of babies (figure 1-2).

Figure 1-2

By the next month, they will have produced a second pair of babies, and the first pair will have matured (figure 1-3).

Figure 1-3

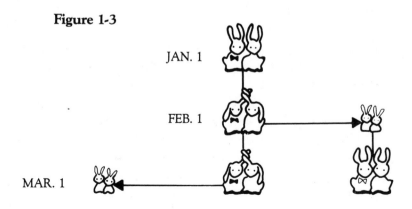

One month later, they will have another new pair of babies, the second pair will have matured, and the first pair will have babies of their own (figure 1-4).

Figure 1-4

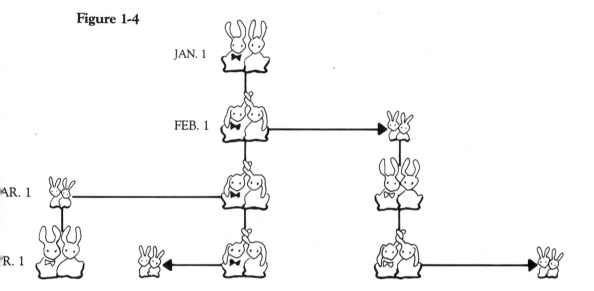

JAN. 1

FEB. 1

AR. 1

R. 1

The drawing can continue as shown in figure 1-5, though it rapidly becomes unmanageable. A tally of the number of pairs of rabbits each month, however, reveals a pattern by which the problem can be solved (see table 1-1). It is not the answer (377 counting the original pair) but rather the pattern 1, 1, 2, 3, 5, 8, 13, . . . that distinguishes the problem. The sequence begins with 1, and each number that follows is the sum of the *previous two numbers.*

0+1   1+1   1+2   2+3   3+5   5+8

1, 1, 2, 3, 5, 8, 13, . . .

Because this work of Fibonacci's is the earliest known recording of this infinite sequence, it has come to be known as the *Fibonacci sequence,* made up of *Fibonacci numbers.* The first 12 Fibonacci numbers are 1, 1, 2, 3, 5, 8, 13, 21, 34, 55, 89, 144.

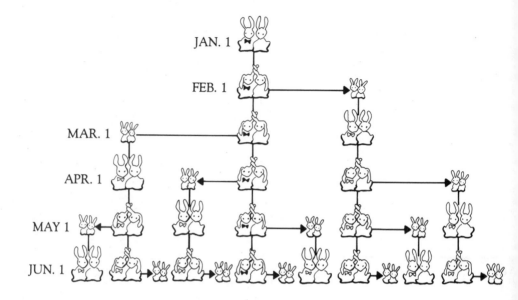

Figure 1-5

The rabbit breeding problem: half a year later, 13 pairs of rabbits.

Table 1-1 Tally of the Pairs of Rabbits by Month

Month	No. of Pairs of Babies	No. of Pairs of Adults	Total No. of Pairs
Jan. 1	0	1	1
Feb. 1	1	1	2
Mar. 1	1	2	3
Apr. 1	2	3	5
May 1	3	5	8
Jun. 1	5	8	13
Jul. 1	8	13	21
Aug. 1	13	21	34
Sep. 1	21	34	55
Oct. 1	34	55	89
Nov. 1	55	89	144
Dec. 1	89	144	233
Jan. 1	144	233	377

A Fibonacci ratio consists of any Fibonacci number divided by another Fibonacci number—typically adjacent in the sequence, the smaller number appearing first. An example of a Fibonacci ratio is 5/8. Sometimes the numbers are not adjacent (5/13), and sometimes the larger appears first (8/5).

The rabbit problem and its solution are contrived (rabbits really don't breed quite that way), but the Fibonacci sequence itself does occur naturally in many other contexts. It appears repeatedly in real, natural phenomena as diverse as pinecones and poems, sunflowers and symphonies, ancient art and modern computers, the solar system and the stock market! Indeed, Fibonacci numbers and ratios appear to be lurking "happily ever after" all over the place, just waiting to be discovered.

CHAPTER 2

Fibonacci Numbers in Nature

One of the most reliable places to look for Fibonacci numbers in nature is in the growth patterns of plants. Plants tend to grow in spirals as they "reach" for moisture, sunlight, and air, which are available somewhat cyclically. That is, as the tip of a branch moves in a circular motion reaching for the elements, it also gets longer because it is growing; the tip spirals in space. Thus, growth spirals are characterized by both a circular motion and elongation.

As a branch grows, it generates leaves at regular intervals but not, typically, after each complete circle of its spiral. One explanation for this is that leaves generated after a complete circle would grow directly above one another and would shelter each other from the very elements they need. It appears that leaves are generated after 2/5 of a circle of growth, or after 3/5 of a circle, or after 3/8, 8/13, 5/13, or other similar fractional parts of a circle of growth. Curiously, these *phyllotactic* ratios, as they are called, are usually Fibonacci ratios—their numerators and denominators are Fibonacci numbers.

An illustration of the phyllotactic ratio 3/8 is shown in figure 2-1. Each stem developed 3/8 of a turn from the previous stem. It took 3 complete turns to generate 8 stems. Phyllotactic ratios can be determined by finding a stem directly above another stem and counting the number of full circle turns the branch went through while generating the stems in between as well as the newest stem. (The original stem is not counted.)

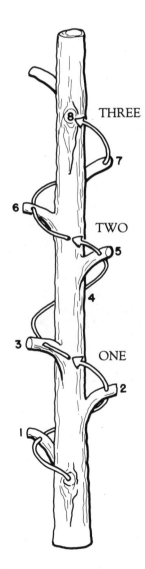

THREE

TWO

ONE

Figure 2-1

Eight stems were produced in three complete growth spirals. This illustrates the phyllotactic ratio 3/8.

NEARLY ALL PHYLLOTACTIC RATIOS ARE FIBONACCI RATIOS!

Here are some examples of phyllotactic ratios:*

Ratio	Plants
2/3	Grasses, elm
1/3	Grasses, blackberry, beech, hazel, fiddleneck
2/5	Mustard, common groundsel, toyon, coast live oak, madrona, California bay, pepper tree, poplar, holly, manzanita, apple, plum, cherry, apricot
3/8	Petty spurge, weeping willow, pear, locust (thorn phyllotaxy)
5/13	Bottlebrush, pussy willow, almond

Long-stemmed plants sometimes generate leaves in one phyllotactic ratio near the bottom of the plant and in a different ratio further up the stem; the new ratio also consists of Fibonacci numbers.†

Fibonacci ratios have been observed in some species of cactus, but less consistently and predictably. Palm tree phyllotaxis reliably exhibits Fibonacci ratios, often dramatically apparent on the trunks of the trees (see figure 2-2).

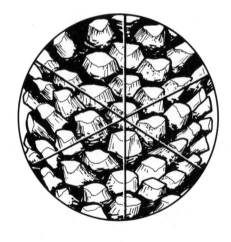

Figure 2-2

Palm tree showing how leaf stubs spiral around the trunk.

---

* 1977 *Yearbook of Science and the Future* (Chicago: Encyclopedia Britannica, 1976), 189.

† Brother Alfred Brousseau, "Fibonacci Numbers in Nature" (Research Report, St. Mary's College, Moraga, CA), 2.

The spirals that characterize pinecones are an even clearer example of Fibonacci ratios. The bracts on the surface of a pinecone are considered modified leaves that have been compressed into a small space. They spiral around the cone much as leaves do around a stem. On close examination, however, two sets of spirals can usually be found, one going diagonally from lower left to upper right and the other crossing it diagonally from lower right to upper left. One spiral rises gradually; the other rises more steeply (see figure 2-3).

Figure 2-3

The pinecone on the right shows one of 13 parallel rows of bracts spiraling steeply.
The pinecone below shows one of 8 parallel rows of bracts spiraling gradually.

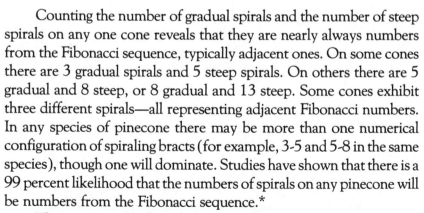

Counting the number of gradual spirals and the number of steep spirals on any one cone reveals that they are nearly always numbers from the Fibonacci sequence, typically adjacent ones. On some cones there are 3 gradual spirals and 5 steep spirals. On others there are 5 gradual and 8 steep, or 8 gradual and 13 steep. Some cones exhibit three different spirals—all representing adjacent Fibonacci numbers. In any species of pinecone there may be more than one numerical configuration of spiraling bracts (for example, 3-5 and 5-8 in the same species), though one will dominate. Studies have shown that there is a 99 percent likelihood that the numbers of spirals on any pinecone will be numbers from the Fibonacci sequence.*

The outer petals of artichokes are positioned in two clear sets of spirals and can be counted in much the same way as the bracts of

* Brousseau, *Fibonacci Numbers in Nature*, 4.

Figure 2-4

The artichoke on the left shows one of 5 parallel rows of petals spiraling gradually. The artichoke on the right shows one of 8 parallel rows of petals spiraling steeply.

pinecones. There are usually 3 gradual and 5 steep or 5 gradual and 8 steep (see figure 2-4). The outer leaves (really the petals) of other flower buds also spiral, typically in adjacent Fibonacci numbers. Dusty miller buds have 5 gradual spirals and 8 steep ones. Cornflowers have 3 gradual and 5 steep.

The outer surface of the pineapple is covered by hexagonally shaped scales. On close examination we can see that any hexagon is on three different spirals, each spiral aligned through opposite sides of the hexagon (see figure 2-5). If we count the number of gradual, medium, and steep spirals on any pineapple, we usually find that there are 8, 13, and 21—adjacent Fibonacci numbers. A study of 2,000 pineapples revealed not one deviation from the Fibonacci pattern.* Sometimes four different Fibonacci spirals can be identified on one pineapple.

Figure 2-5

The first pineapple shows one of 8 parallel rows of scales spiraling gradually. The next pineapple shows one of 13 parallel rows of scales spiraling at a medium slope. The last pineapple shows one of 21 parallel rows of scales spiraling steeply.

---

* *1977 Yearbook of Science and the Future*, 188.

Sunflowers display Fibonacci numbers in their own unique way. If we look directly into the center of the head of a mature sunflower, we can observe two distinctly different spirals of seeds, one going clockwise and the other going counterclockwise, as shown in figure 2-6. The usual number of spirals in a sunflower head is 34 going one way and 55 going the other. Giant sunflowers have 55 going one way and 89 going the other. Other sunflowers have been reported to have 89 and 144, or 144 and 233. All of these are, of course, adjacent Fibonacci numbers. While occasional deviations can be found, studies have revealed sunflower spirals to be overwhelmingly Fibonaccian. Sometimes the numbers are double Fibonacci; for example, rather than 34, 55, the numbers will be 68, 110.

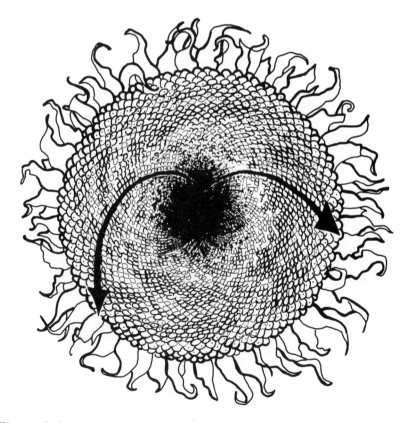

Figure 2-6

Head of a sunflower showing one of 55 parallel rows of seeds spiraling counterclockwise and one of 89 parallel rows of seeds spiraling clockwise.

Many flowers exhibit Fibonacci numbers not only in their buds and seeds, but also in the count of their petals. Most daisies have 13, 21, or 34 petals. Anyone playing " . . . loves me, . . . loves me not" with the petals of a daisy will pull off a Fibonacci number of petals before arriving at an answer.

Counting the number of petals of many other flowers reveals Fibonacci numbers, as shown below*:

Petal Count	Plants
2	Enchanter's nightshade
3	Lily, iris
5	Wall lettuce, buttercup, wild rose, larkspur, columbine
8	Squalid senecio, field senecio, cosmos, delphiniums, bloodroot
13	Ragwort, corn marigold, mayweed, cineraria, double delphiniums
21	Heleniums, aster, black-eyed susan, chicory, hawkbits
34	Field daisies, plantain, pyrethrums
55	African daisies, heleniums, Michaelmas daisies
89	Michaelmas daisies

It is notable that although some flowers virtually always display the same number of petals (iris and buttercup, for example), others have what should simply be called a strong tendency toward a specific number. Among daisies, for example, there are some 13-petaled varieties that generate flowers in the 11- to 15-petal range. However, most will be 13, most deviants will be near 13, and the average of the species as a whole will be 13. If petal counts and other manifestations of phyllotaxis do not follow an absolute "law," they do, in the words of one investigator, exhibit a "fascinatingly prevalent tendency" to be Fibonaccian.†

Fibonacci numbers can also be observed in the way some plants branch as they grow. An ideally simplified diagram of a plant branching with the passing of time is shown in figure 2-7. Initially there is one stem that branches into two. One of these new stems branches again while the other delays doing so. This is repeated each time a stem branches; one branches and the other waits. At each horizontal level

---

* 1977 Yearbook of Science and the Future, 187.

†H. S. M. Coxeter, Introduction to Geometry (New York: John Wiley & Sons, 1961), 172.

Figure 2-7

Sneezewort (*Achillea ptarmica*), showing number of stems at each horizontal level of development. (Adapted with permission from E. H. Huntley, *The Divine Proportion*, 163.)

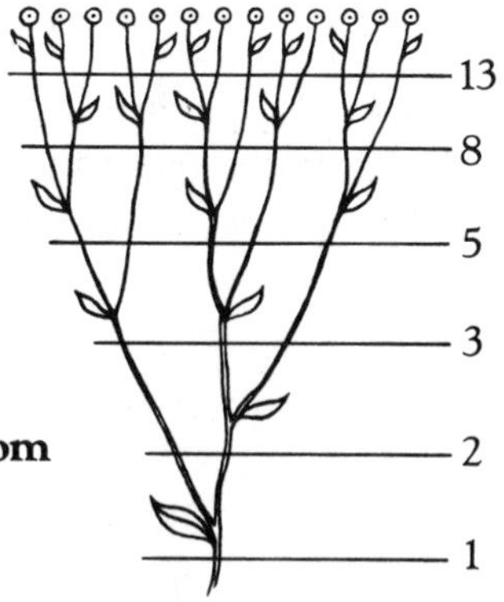

the number of stems is a Fibonacci number. Perfect specimens are hard to find, since this process is subject to stressful environmental influences. But some trees, root systems, and algae do appear to exhibit this "Fibonacci branching pattern."

A similar set of events resulting in the same sequence of numbers characterizes the family tree of a male bee. A male bee develops from an unfertilized egg; to put it more simply, a male bee has only a mother, not a father. A female bee, on the other hand, develops from a fertilized egg and therefore has both a mother and a father. The symbolic representation of the genealogy of a male bee is shown in figure 2-8. The female parentage always branches into two; the male does not.

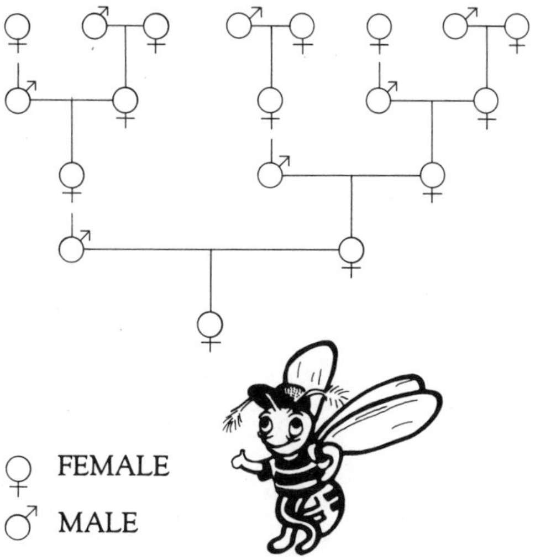

ANCESTORS

Male	Female	Total No.
3	5	8
2	3	5
1	2	3
1	1	2
0	1	1

♀ FEMALE

♂ MALE

Figure 2-8

Genealogy of a male bee.

Clearly, then, Fibonacci numbers are associated with animals as well as plants. One of the most fascinating examples of the sequence in the animal kingdom is the remarkable spiral that characterizes some animal growth. This spiral can be constructed as shown in figure 2-9.

Figure 2-9
Construction of an equiangular spiral.

1. Begin with a 1-unit square.

☒

2. Attach another 1-unit square to it.

☒

3. Attach a 2-unit square where it fits.

| 2 | ☒ |

4. Attach a 3-unit square where it fits.

| 2 | ☒ |
| 3 | |

5. In like fashion (continuing in the same direction), attach squares of 5, 8, 13, 21, and 34 units.

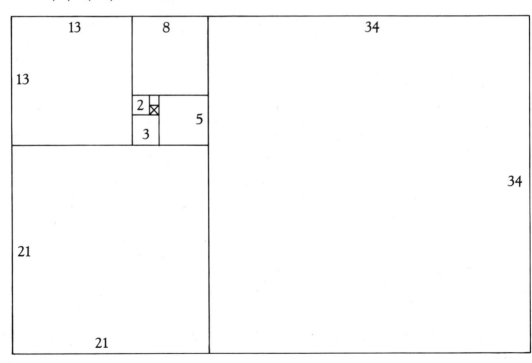

Construction could, of course, continue as far as space permitted, with squares of exactly the needed dimension being added successively. Then quarter-circle arcs can be drawn connecting opposite corners of the squares (using the sides as the radii of the arcs) in such a way that the arcs connect sequentially (see figure 2-10).

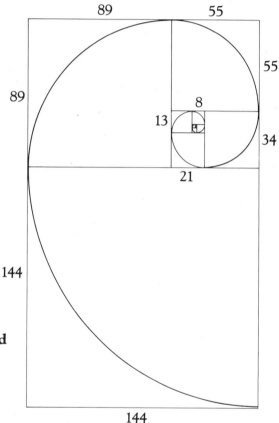

Figure 2-10

Equiangular spiral approximated using Fibonacci proportions.

What develops is a close approximation of a beautiful spiral, known variously as an equiangular or logarithmic spiral. Visually it can be described as a long, slow spiral. It is quite different from a more "evenly spaced" spiral, as represented, for example, by the groove on a phonograph record and known as an Archimedian spiral. The building blocks of this particular spiral are squares whose dimensions are successive terms in the Fibonacci sequence. It is called an equiangular spiral because all radii from its center intersect the spiral itself at exactly the same angle.

Perhaps the clearest and loveliest example of an equiangular spiral is the shell of the chambered nautilus. As a nautilus grows, it is necessary for the chamber in which it lives to become larger (to accommodate its increased size) yet stay the same shape (to accommodate the contour of its body). An examination of the cross section of the shell shows how this is done (see figure 2-11). As the shell gets larger, the radii also get larger, but the angles of intersection of the radii and the outer shell remain the same. Therefore, the chambers will be similarly shaped but larger. Each time this happens, the living nautilus moves into new, familiar, but roomier quarters, where it lives comfortably until the process needs to be repeated.

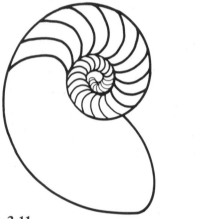 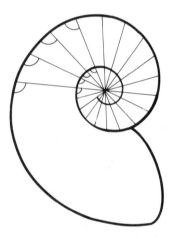

Figure 2-11
On the left is a cross section of a chambered nautilus shell. On the right is a diagram of the shell showing the intersection of the radii and the shell at equal angles.

Many equiangular spirals can be found in the animal kingdom; examples include the horns of wild sheep, spider webs, parrot beaks, cat and canary claws, elephant tusks, the graph of bacterial growth, and the path of an insect approaching light. Most of these occurrences seem to be linked to the basic characteristic of the spiral—retaining the same shape while getting larger. Although not all equiangular spirals exhibit the Fibonacci proportions, many do, and others (such as animal horns) appear to but are difficult to verify because they do not lie in a plane. At present one can only speculate on the full scope of the spiral's occurrence in nature.

Fibonacci numbers also play a role in regular pentagons, of which there is an abundance in nature. More flowers bloom in pentagons than in any other shape. The sand dollar, the sea urchin, and the starfish are examples of pentagons found in the sea. The insides of fruits and vegetables are often pentagonal in shape (see figure 2-12).

The proportions of a pentagon approximate the proportions between adjacent Fibonacci numbers; the higher the numbers are, the more exact the approximation becomes. For example, if the measure of the side of a pentagon is a Fibonacci number, the measure of its diagonal is the next Fibonacci number in the sequence. Furthermore,

Figure 2-12

Four of nature's pentagons. (Reprinted with permission from LeRoy C. Dalton, *Algebra in the Real World*, 186–87.)

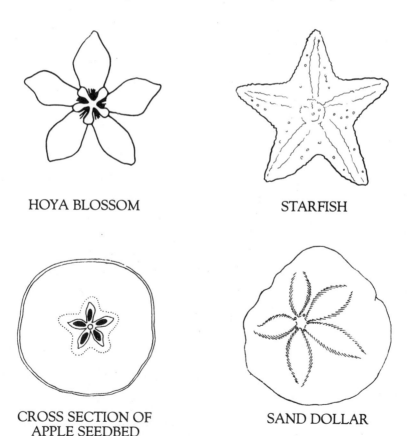

HOYA BLOSSOM

STARFISH

CROSS SECTION OF
APPLE SEEDBED

SAND DOLLAR

the diagonals of any such pentagon separate each other into two adjacent Fibonacci numbers. These principles are illustrated in figure 2-13 with the Fibonacci numbers 55, 89, and 144.

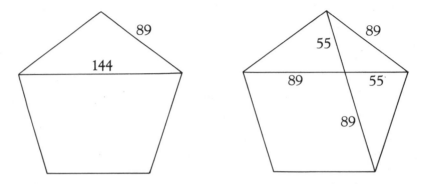

Figure 2-13

The pentagon on the left shows Fibonacci proportions in the sides and diagonals. The pentagon on the right shows the diagonals intersecting in Fibonacci proportions.

Occurrences of the Fibonacci sequence in nature—like the sequence itself—seem never to end. Pine needles tend to grow in clusters of 2, 3, or 5, depending on the species. The number of chambers in many plant pods is a Fibonacci number. The mathematics of snowflake construction yields a Fibonacci ratio. Much the same way that bracts spiral around a pinecone—in Fibonacci configurations—the units of protein spiral around the flagella (tails) of single-celled organisms as they swim (an observation that can only be made with an electron microscope).

The search for additional natural occurrences of the Fibonacci sequence can be a source of endless curiosity and infinite satisfaction.

CHAPTER 3

Fibonacci Numbers in Art and Architecture

Fibonacci numbers and ratios have had a curious influence on art and architecture for many centuries. There seems to be a visually pleasing quality to these numbers and their relationship to each other that has appealed to humanity's sense of beauty since the beginning of recorded history. Today, the popularity of 3-by-5- and 5-by-8-inch index cards and booklets is simple testimonial to the appeal of Fibonacci proportions, 3, 5, and 8 being Fibonacci numbers. Similar proportions characterize playing cards, writing pads, windows, post-cards, cabinets, mirrors, light switch plates, calculators, and credit cards, to mention only a few items in an endless list of Fibonaccian shapes that are found everywhere.

In fact, these shapes are close approximations of a very special rectangle that most people seem unconsciously to favor—so special that is has come to be known as the "golden rectangle." It strikes people as quite perfect, being neither too fat and stubby nor too long and skinny. It lies somewhere between a square and a double square—

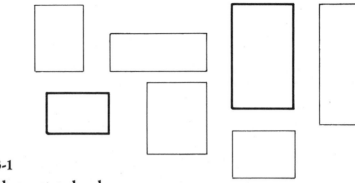

Figure 3-1

**Two golden rectangles shown among
rectangles of differing proportions.**

not exactly in the middle, but a little closer to the double square (see
figure 3-1).

About 100 years ago, German psychologist Gustav Fechner
measured the dimensions of thousands of common rectangles and
found that, on the average, their proportions tended to be close to the
golden rectangle. He also tested hundreds of people to determine their
preference for rectangles and found the average choice generally to be
close to the golden rectangle. Over the years this fact has been heavily
exploited by the advertising and retailing businesses in labels, ads,
packages, and displays.

Fechner also conducted exhaustive studies of the crosses in
graveyards and discovered an interesting relationship between the

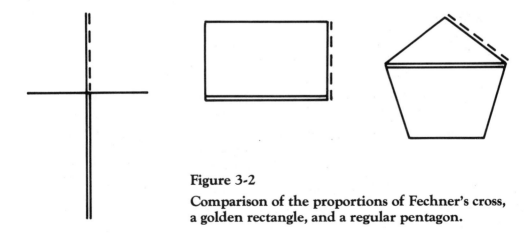

Figure 3-2

**Comparison of the proportions of Fechner's cross,
a golden rectangle, and a regular pentagon.**

crosses and the golden rectangle. The main stem of the crosses tended to be cut by the cross bar in the same proportion as that found in the sides of the golden rectangle. This happens also to be the same proportion that exists between a side and a diagonal of a regular pentagon (see figure 3-2).

This proportion has intrigued mathematicians, artists, and architects for over 4,000 years. It appears to have been a factor in the building of the Great Pyramid of Gizeh in Egypt 4,600 years ago. The Greeks had a name for it 2,300 years ago—the "golden ratio." In medieval times people considered it an expression of God's purpose. They referred to it as the "divine proportion," reflecting the belief in its relation to the will of God.

This proportion has many unique qualities. If the small part is called S and the large part is called L, the proportion can be stated mathematically as follows:

$$\frac{S}{L} = \frac{L}{S+L}$$

More simply, the ratio of the small to the large is the same as the ratio of the large to the total. In the case of the cross, the relationship between the small top and the large bottom is the same as the relationship between the large bottom and the entire main stem, as shown in figure 3-3. Sometimes the proportion is called the "golden section"; the word *section* means "cut"—in just exactly the right place

Figure 3-3
Small : large = large : whole.

$$\frac{AB}{BC} = \frac{BC}{AC}$$

or

$$\frac{S}{L} = \frac{L}{S+L}$$

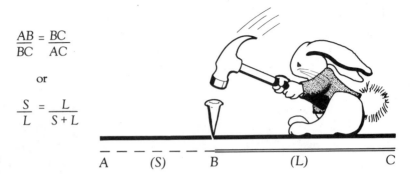

A   (S)   B   (L)   C

Figure 3-4
The golden section (cut).

so that the small is to the large as the large is to the whole (see figure 3-4).

The relationship that exists between the two sides of the golden rectangle can be expressed similarly: the small side is to the large as the large is to the sum of the two sides. But another unique characteristic emerges in the rectangle. If a square is cut away from one end of the rectangle, the remaining rectangle has the golden proportion. If a square is cut away from that smaller rectangle, the new rectangle is also "golden," and so on without end. There is, of course, only one very specific rectangle about which this could be true (see figure 3-5).

Mathematicians have examined the proportions of such a rectangle and have determined that if the large side is 1, the small side is 0.618034 . . . . If the small side is 1, the large side is 1.618034 . . . .

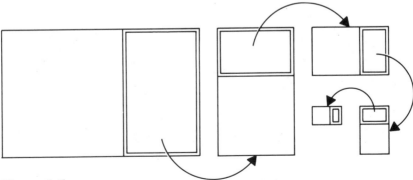

Figure 3-5
Golden rectangles within golden rectangles.

An examination of the decimal equivalents of Fibonacci ratios soon reveals an inclination toward the same values, plus (+) or minus (−):

Ratios Less Than 1				Ratios Greater Than 1		
1/1	= 1.000000	(+)		1/1	= 1.000000	(−)
1/2	= 0.500000	(−)		2/1	= 2.000000	(+)
2/3	= 0.666666 . . .(+)			3/2	= 1.500000	(−)
3/5	= 0.600000	(−)		5/3	= 1.666666 . . .(+)	
5/8	= 0.625000	(+)		8/5	= 1.600000	(−)
8/13	= 0.615384 . . .(−)			13/8	= 1.625000	(+)
13/21	= 0.619047 . . .(+)			21/13	= 1.615384 . . .(−)	
21/34	= 0.617647 . . .(−)			34/21	= 1.619047 . . .(+)	
34/55	= 0.618181 . . .(+)			55/34	= 1.617647 . . .(−)	
55/89	= 0.617977 . . .(−)			89/55	= 1.618181 . . .(+)	
89/144	= 0.618055 . . .(+)			144/89	= 1.617977 . . .(−)	
144/233	= 0.618025 . . .(−)			233/144	= 1.618055 . . .(+)	
233/377	= 0.618037 . . .(+)			377/233	= 1.618025 . . .(−)	

The further along in the sequence the ratios are, the closer the decimal equivalent comes to 0.618034 . . . . In fact, the values alternate between being a little greater than (+) and a little less than (−) the exact value. With each successive ratio the difference becomes smaller. It is as if the Fibonacci numbers were trying deliberately to be in golden ratio to each other—overshooting or undershooting slightly but getting increasingly closer to the perfect ratio.

It is said that these values "converge" to the golden ratio 0.618034 . . . , which can be proved to be the irrational number $(\sqrt{5} - 1)/2$. This special number is frequently referred to as "phi," symbolically represented as Φ. Although there is no accurate decimal equivalent for any irrational number, 0.618 is about as exact as the ratio needs to be for most purposes. The simple ratio 5/8 (0.625) is a workable approximation and is used for many practical purposes today; 8/13, of course, is closer, and 13/21 is closer still.

The Great Pyramid of Gizeh in Egypt, built in about 2600 BC, is the earliest known example of the golden ratio in architecture. The ratio of the altitude to the length of one side of the square base is about

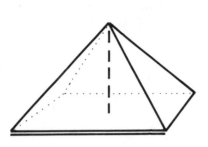 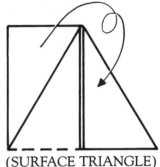

(SURFACE TRIANGLE)

Figure 3-6

Proportions of the Great Pyramid of Gizeh.

5 to 8, or 0.625. Furthermore, the triangular sides are believed to be golden rectangles that have been cut along a diagonal and rejoined along the long sides (see figure 3-6).

Additional intriguing facts about the Great Pyramid include at least one scholarly report that the Egyptians, who are believed to have worked in inches, built the pyramid to an original height of 5,813 inches (recall that 5, 8, and 13 are Fibonacci numbers).* This is difficult to verify because the capstones have crumbled somewhat over the years. Curiously, the area of the base today is reported to be 13 hectares, or 8 acres. Hectares and acres are the units of land area of the two principal measuring systems in use in the world today, metric and English respectively.

Evidence of the use of the golden rectangle in architecture can be found throughout history and all over the world; sometimes the evidence is concealed, other times more obvious. It is buried deeply inside the tomb of Ramses IV, built in Egypt 1,400 years after the Great Pyramid. The burial chamber consists of three rectangles, a small one inside a middle-sized one inside a large one. The small one is a double square, the middle one is a golden rectangle, and the large one is a double golden rectangle (see figure 3-7).

The exterior dimensions of the Parthenon in Athens, built in about 440 BC, form a perfect golden rectangle, and the proportion can be found elsewhere in that structure (see figure 3-8). The Greeks

*William Hoffer, "A Magic Ratio Occurs Throughout Art and Nature," *Smithsonian*, December 1975, 115.

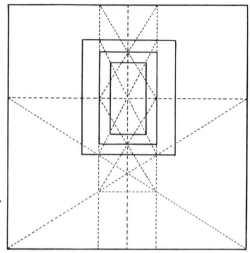

Figure 3-7
Floor plan of the tomb of Ramses IV.
(Reprinted with permission from
Matila Ghyka, *The Geometry of Art*
and Life, **plate LVIII.)**

appear to have been strongly influenced by golden proportions, consciously or unconsciously, since the classical age of Greek culture beginning in the fifth century BC. Geometric analysis of Greek statues and artifacts, such as vases, urns, and so on, clearly reveals extensive use of the golden ratio (see figure 3-9). It is for Phidias, considered the greatest of Greek sculptors, that the golden ratio was named "phi"; the proportion can be found abundantly in his work, including the bands of sculpture that run above the columns of the Parthenon.

Much of Renaissance art and architecture was inspired by the Greek sense of beauty and proportion. It is not surprising, then, that so

Figure 3-8

Golden rectangle and golden proportions
in the Parthenon.

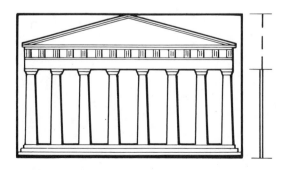

Figure 3-9
Greek urn in golden
rectangle.

many buildings, statues, and tombs of that prolific era are characterized by golden ratios—doorways, floor plans, windows, gates, overall dimensions, and so on.

Today, the presence of golden proportions in contemporary architecture is not an accident. The famous twentieth-century architect Le Corbusier was deeply committed to the use of golden proportions in his work. His influence can be found in buildings ranging from private villas in France to the headquarters of the United Nations in New York City (see figure 3-10). He is not alone; other architects use the golden proportion to greater or lesser extents.

The "divine proportion," as Leonardo da Vinci called it, also figures prominently in the works of many great painters. The golden rectangle itself can often be found in a painting, as shown in figure 3-11. The proportion may exist in some other form—simple exterior

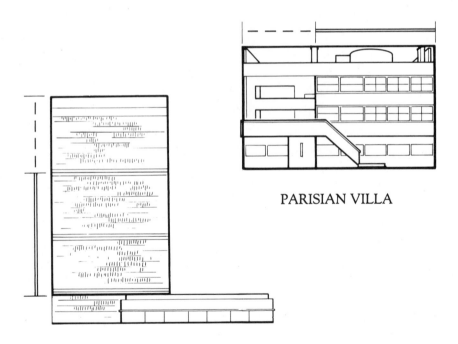

PARISIAN VILLA

UNITED NATIONS BUILDING

Figure 3-10
Golden rectangles in modern architecture.

Figure 3-11

**Golden rectangle in Giotto's *Madonna
Enshrined with Saints*, c. 1300.**

dimensions, for example, or an underlying grid (see figure 3-12). A
collection of such paintings would include representatives from
virtually all traditions and styles, ranging from the old masters to
modern artists. The late nineteenth-century French impressionist artist
Seurat is said to have "attacked every canvas with the golden
rectangle." Dürer, Mondrian, and Bellows are other artists who are
known to have consciously incorporated the golden ratio into their
work.

0.618	1.0
0.618	1.0

1.618

Figure 3-12

Golden proportions in exterior dimensions and underlying grid of a contemporary landscape painting, *Wood Ranch Portrait*, by Shirley Nootbaar, 1986. (Photograph courtesy of the artist.)

Figure 3-13

Golden proportions in Asian art.

Golden proportions can easily be identified in art objects from around the world. The exterior dimensions of a seated Buddha from India dating from the third century, shown in figure 3-13, exhibit these proportions, as does the shape of a bowl traced to the Ching dynasty of China, also shown in figure 3-13. Floor mosaics in ancient temples in Syria feature golden proportions. It appears that mosaic artists used the same exact dimensions over and over again and that a measuring device must have existed to allow them to do this. Scholars have determined that a ruler divided into golden proportions would fit the mosaic patterns exactly (see figure 3-14), explaining why the same dimensions can be found in widely separated geographic areas of ancient civilization.

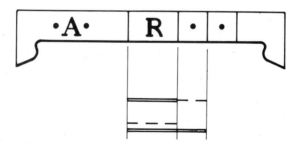

Figure 3-14

Golden proportions in ruler used to lay mosaics. (Adapted with permission from Richard E. M. Moore, "Mosaic Units," *Fibonacci Quarterly* 8, p. 309.)

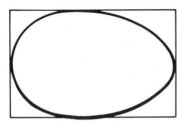

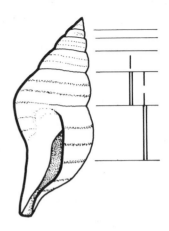

Figure 3-15
Chicken egg in a golden rectangle and the golden proportion in a shell.

Curiously, golden proportions are clearly visible in nature's art and architecture. The average chicken egg, for example, fits nicely inside a golden rectangle; the golden ratio can be found in the cross section of certain kinds of shells (see figure 3-15). Many evergreen trees grow in the shape of golden rectangles; the principal veining of some leaves reveals golden proportions (see figure 3-16). One equiangular spiral prevalent in nature is often called the "golden spiral." It fits nicely inside a rectangle that can be constructed with Fibonacci dimensioned squares, as illustrated in figure 2-9. It can be observed in the shape of some plants as they grow and others as they die, in some animal horns and sea shells, and in the configuration of ocean waves, galaxies, water currents, and storms (see figure 3-17).

Figure 3-16
Norway spruce in a golden rectangle and the golden proportion in an ivy leaf.

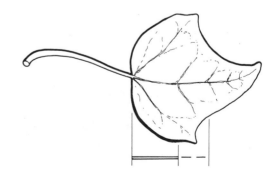

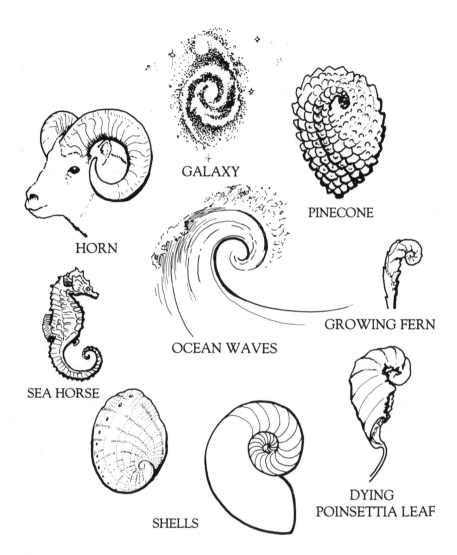

GALAXY

PINECONE

HORN

OCEAN WAVES

GROWING FERN

SEA HORSE

DYING
POINSETTIA LEAF

SHELLS

Figure 3-17
Equiangular spirals in nature.

The apparent link between nature's proportions and the proportions found in art and architecture has been pondered by philosophers over the years. Something called "dynamic symmetry" is understood to operate in many shapes and forms characterized by harmonious but unequal proportions that are pleasing to the human eye. The dynamic symmetry of a pinecone or egg differs from the static symmetry of a marble. Static symmetry is characterized by sameness and can result in monotony. An object with dynamic symmetry can be said to have "variety and unity," meaning it is interesting and goes together as a whole. Many fine artists and great architects distinguish themselves by the ability to pull together carefully constructed elements of varying proportions into units that are vibrant with movement.

It has been suggested that the golden ratio might be an underlying explanation for what we call "beauty" both in a natural object and in an artistic masterpiece. Perhaps there is a common thread of proportion and balance running through all of nature, including the thoughts and feelings of human beings.

CHAPTER 4

Fibonacci Numbers in Music and Poetry

Perhaps the clearest link between Fibonacci numbers and music can be found on the keyboard of a piano. An octave on a keyboard is made up of 8 white keys and 5 black keys. The black keys are positioned in groups of 2 and 3. There are 13 keys altogether in one octave, an analysis of which involves each of the first six Fibonacci numbers (see figure 4-1).

The keyboard aside, those 13 notes belong to what is known as the chromatic scale, the most complete scale to have developed in Western music. Its principal predecessor was the 8-note diatonic scale, better known as the octave, which was preceded by the 5-note pentatonic scale. The pentatonic scale was used in early European music and is the basis today of the American Kodaly method of music education for young children. Any 5 consecutive black keys on a keyboard constitute such a scale. A number of well-known folk tunes can be played using just these keys; examples include "Mary Had a Little Lamb," "Ring Around the Rosy," "Go Tell It on the Mountain,"

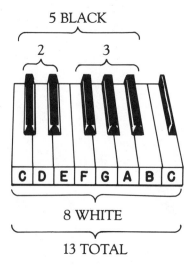

5 BLACK

2   3

C D E F G A B C

8 WHITE

13 TOTAL

Figure 4-1

Fibonacci numbers in an octave on the piano.

and "Amazing Grace." Although other scales have existed, the pentatonic (5), diatonic (8), and chromatic (13) scales dominate the development of Western music (see figure 4-2).

The musical intervals considered by many to be the most pleasing to the ear are the major sixth and minor sixth. A major sixth, for example, consists of C, vibrating at about 264 vibrations per second, and A, vibrating at about 440 vibrations per second. The ratio of 264 to 440 reduces to 3/5, a Fibonacci ratio (see figure 4-3). An example of a minor sixth would be E (about 330 vibrations per second) and C (about 528 vibrations per second). That ratio, 330 to 528, reduces to 5/8, the next Fibonacci ratio. The vibrations of any sixth interval reduce to a similar ratio. It has been suggested that the Fibonacci numbers are part of a natural harmony that not only looks good to the eye but sounds good to the ear.

Perhaps this is why composers have consciously or unconsciously incorporated Fibonacci numbers and proportions into their works. Scholarly analyses of a wide range of music including Gregorian chants, Bach fugues, and Bartók sonatas reveal this to be true.

Fibonacci numbers function in a variety of ways in musical compositions. Perhaps the most important of these is the division of musical time into periods whose lengths are in the same ratio to each other as the Fibonacci ratios. Just as an artist will take a blank easel and

Figure 4-2

The scale in the development of Western music.

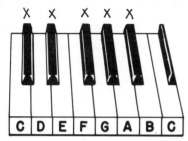

1. PENTATONIC SCALE (5 NOTES)

Old Folk Tunes:
"Mary Had a Little Lamb"
"Ring Around the Rosy"
"Go Tell It on the Mountain"
"Amazing Grace"

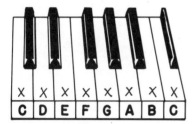

2. DIATONIC SCALE (8 NOTES)

Simple, Classic Melodies:
Brahms's "Lullaby"
"Row, Row, Row Your Boat"
"Are You Sleeping?"
"Hickory Dickory Dock"

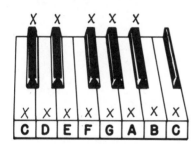

3. CHROMATIC SCALE (13 NOTES)

Most Music Today,
Including Great Symphonies
and Contemporary Music

Figure 4-3

Fibonacci ratios in musical intervals.

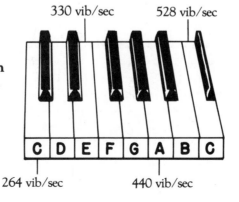

330 vib/sec   528 vib/sec   Minor Sixth

$$\frac{330}{528} = \frac{5}{8}$$

264 vib/sec   440 vib/sec

$$\frac{264}{440} = \frac{3}{5}$$

Major Sixth

divide it into areas based on the golden proportion to determine the placement of horizons, trees and so on, a composer will divide musical time into periods based on that same proportion to determine the beginnings and endings of themes, moods, textures, and so on. One way to do this is to use Fibonacci numbers to group measures together (see figure 4-4).

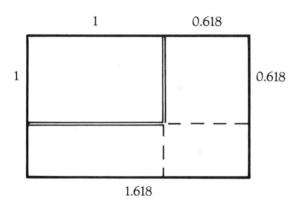

Figure 4-4

The golden proportion applied by an artist to space in painting, and similarly applied by a composer to time in music.

Entire Composition

		0.618	1
34 measures	55 measures	21 measures	34 measures
0.618	1		

| Theme | Slow, soft | Fast, loud | Repeat of theme |

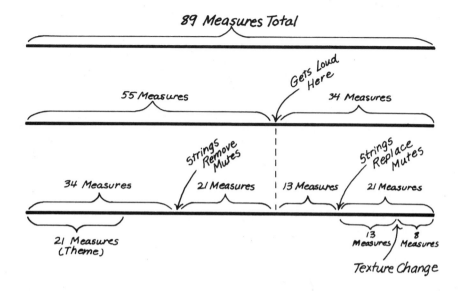

Figure 4-5

First movement, Music for Strings, Percussion, and Celeste, by Béla Bartók. (Adapted with permission from Erno Landavi, *Béla Bartók, An Analysis of His Music*, 28, 29.)

This technique has been identified in compositions ranging from early church music to modern masterpieces, including works of Palestrina, Bach, Beethoven, and Bartók.* As an example of the division of musical time into Fibonacci parts, figure 4-5 shows a diagram of the first movement of Bartók's Music for Strings, Percussion, and Celeste.

Beethoven achieved the golden proportion in his famous Fifth Symphony by the strategic placement of the well-known motto shown in figure 4-6.

Figure 4-6

---

* *1977 Yearbook of Science and the Future*, 191.

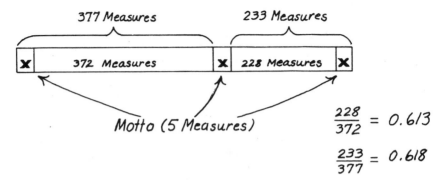

Figure 4-7

First movement of Beethoven's Fifth Symphony divided into golden proportions by the motto.

The three main occurrences of the motto divide the first movement according to the golden section. If the first and last mottos are considered along with the intervening measures, the middle motto divides the entire movement into Fibonacci proportions (see figure 4-7).

Fibonacci numbers are also used by some composers to aid in the development of a melody line. The highly mathematical Schillinger system of musical composition suggests that successive notes in a melody be successive Fibonacci units above or below each other, or successive Fibonacci units above or below the beginning note, or some other variation of Fibonacci intervals between notes (see figure 4-8). Joseph Schillinger, a professor of both mathematics and music at Columbia University in the 1930s, believed that the melody resulting from Fibonaccian jumps in the scale was just as natural as the growth formation of seeds in a sunflower or leaves on a stem. He typically applied only the first few numbers of the Fibonacci sequence, however, because they rapidly become too extreme. Some modern composers do use the extreme numbers to achieve "far-out" effects.

Fibonacci numbers are occasionally used to develop an unusual or unique rhythm in music. Whether in rhythm, melody, or overall proportions, however, listeners are unlikely to be aware of Fibonacci numbers as they go by. Listeners will probably sense a certain balance, a feeling of "rightness" about the musical events they hear and the intriguing patterns formed in the music. Fibonacci numbers serve a useful and worthwhile purpose in any of these contexts.

KEY
1 = ½ step
2 = 1 step
3 = 1½ steps
and so on.

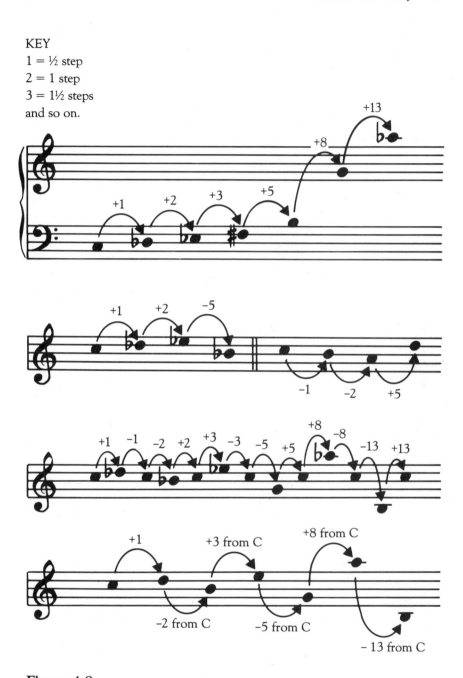

Figure 4-8

Examples of Fibonacci intervals between notes in melodies. (Adapted with permission from Joseph Schillinger, *The Schillinger System of Musical Composition*, 334, 337, 339, 341.)

It is not difficult to find Fibonacci numbers in poetry. Consider, for example, the limerick, made up of 5 lines with a total of 13 beats grouped in 3's and 2's.

A fly and a flea in a flue	*3 beats*
Were imprisoned, so what could they do?	*3 beats*
Said the fly, "Let us flee!"	*2 beats* *5 lines*
"Let us fly!" said the flea,	*2 beats*
So they fled through a flaw in the flue.	*3 beats*
	13 beats

A far more sophisticated example is Virgil's *Aeneid*, the epic Roman poem written in about 20 BC. This literary masterpiece was analyzed in the 1960s by Professor G. E. Duckworth of Princeton University, who discovered frequent use of the Fibonacci sequence to create golden proportions. Other poets of Virgil's time also used these proportions to structure their poems.* Ancient poetry was intended to be heard because only the elite were educated enough to read it. It is not surprising, then, that the harmony and mathematical balance of music should be found in poetry as well; both strive to be pleasing to the ear.

---

*A. F. Horadam, "Further Appearance of the Fibonacci Sequence," *Fibonacci Quarterly* 1 (December 1963): 42.

CHAPTER 5

Fibonacci Numbers in Science and Technology

A sequence of Fibonacci numbers or ratios is one of many patterns researchers find in the data generated by scientific endeavors. These include studies of such diverse phenomena as electrical networks, the reproductive habits of diatoms (tiny water organisms), the basic asymmetries of atoms, and the chemical makeup of pulses traveling along nerve fibers. If scientists are able to find predictable patterns in their work, they really don't need to extend their experiments further; mathematical calculations or logic will yield the desired answers.

The hypothetical examination of rabbit breeding described in chapter 1 provides a perfect case in point. Fibonacci wished to determine how many pairs of rabbits would be in an enclosure a year after the original pair entered, assuming that a pair of rabbits produce another single pair exactly two months after their own birth and every month thereafter (see figure 5-1). Using diagrams and numbers, we see

Figure 5-1

Diagram of the rabbit breeding problem.

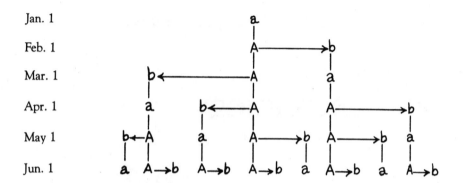

KEY

a = pair of young adult rabbits
A = pair of breeding adult rabbits
b = pair of baby rabbits

		Total Number of Pairs
Jan. 1		1
Feb. 1		2
Mar. 1		3
Apr. 1		5
May 1		8
Jun. 1		13
Jul. 1		21
Aug. 1		34
Sep. 1		55
Oct. 1		89
Nov. 1		144
Dec. 1		233
Jan. 1	(1 year)	377
.	.	.
.	.	.
.	.	.
	2 years	c. 100,000
	3 years	c. 40,000,000
	30 years	c. 2.0×10^{75}
	40 years	c. 2.4×10^{100}

a familiar pattern by the end of the first half-year, from which valid conclusions can be drawn. Not only will there be 377 rabbits a year later, but there will be over 100,000 two years later and nearly 40,000,000 after three years. It has been pointed out that Fibonacci's rabbits will quickly outrun any conceivable food supply or any imaginable enclosure. Isaac Asimov has observed that "in thirty years there would be more rabbits than there are subatomic particles in the known universe, and in forty years there would be more than a googol [10 to the 100th power] of rabbits."* This assumes, of course, that none of them die—which, mercifully, they do!

Other examples can be drawn from almost any field of science. Consider a simple study in optics, a branch of physics. If two glass plates are mounted face-to-face, four interior reflective surfaces exist, labeled 1, 2, 3, and 4 in figure 5-2.

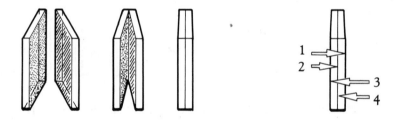

Figure 5-2

There is only one path a ray of light will follow through these glass plates if there are no reflections off any of the surfaces (figure 5-3).

Figure 5-3

---

*Isaac Asimov, *Asimov on Numbers* (New York: Doubleday & Company, 1977), 49.

If a ray is reflected once, there are two paths it can follow, and two different rays will emerge (figure 5-4).

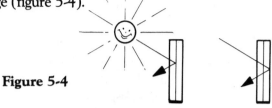

Figure 5-4

If a ray is reflected twice, there are three paths it can follow, with three rays emerging (figure 5-5).

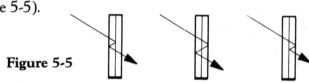

Figure 5-5

If a ray is reflected three times, there are five paths it can follow (figure 5-6).

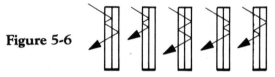

Figure 5-6

If a ray is reflected four times, there are eight paths it can follow (figure 5-7).

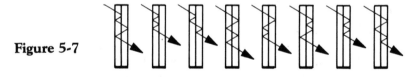

Figure 5-7

If a ray is reflected five times, there are thirteen distinctly different paths it can follow, and thirteen rays will emerge (figure 5-8).

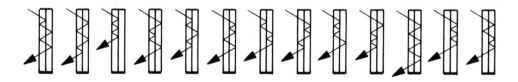

Figure 5-8

All of the above information could be summarized in the following chart:

No. of Reflections	No. of Paths (Rays)
0	1
1	2
2	3
3	5
4	8
5	13
.	.
.	.
.	.

Beyond the point at which a pattern becomes clear, predictions can be made about the number of paths a ray of light will follow as it passes through two glass plates relative to the number of times it will reflect off the surfaces. If, for example, a ray reflected 25 times, the Fibonacci sequence would indicate that there would be 196,418 distinctly different paths it could take and that 196,418 different rays would emerge.

Fibonacci numbers are also found when we examine the possible histories of an electron in an atom of hydrogen gas. Electrons pass through three different states depending on their energy levels, state 0, state 1, and state 2. The following rules apply as an electron gains or loses energy:

- When energy is *gained* (+), electrons in state 1 rise to state 2. Half the electrons in state 0 rise to state 1, and the other half rise to state 2.

- When energy is *lost* (−), electrons in state 1 fall to state 0. Half the electrons in state 2 fall to state 1, and the other half fall to state 0.

This could be summarized as shown in figure 5-9.

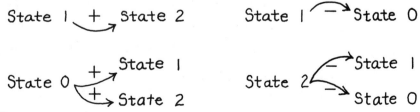

Figure 5-9

Here, then, is a representation of the different possible histories of an electron. After an initial energy gain, the situation shown in figure 5-10 exists. The subsequent energy loss produces the situation shown in figure 5-11. The results of the next energy gain can be seen in figure

Figure 5-10

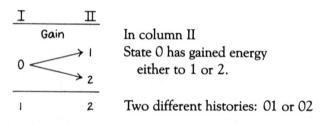

In column II
State 0 has gained energy
   either to 1 or 2.

Two different histories: 01 or 02

Figure 5-11

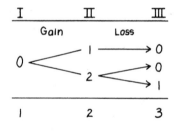

In column III
State 1 has lost energy to 0.
State 2 has lost energy
   either to 0 or 1.

Three different histories: 010, 020, or 021

Figure 5-12

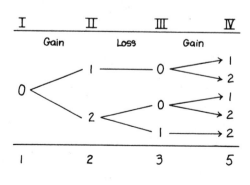

In column IV
State 0 has gained energy
   either to 1 or 2.
The second state 0 has gained
   energy either to 1 or 2.
State 1 has gained energy to 2.

Five different histories:
0101, 0102, 0201, 0202, 0212

5-12. For any given "generation," the number of possible histories is a Fibonacci number, as shown in figure 5-13. Furthermore, the ratio of different states at any point is a Fibonacci ratio, as can be seen in figure 5-14.

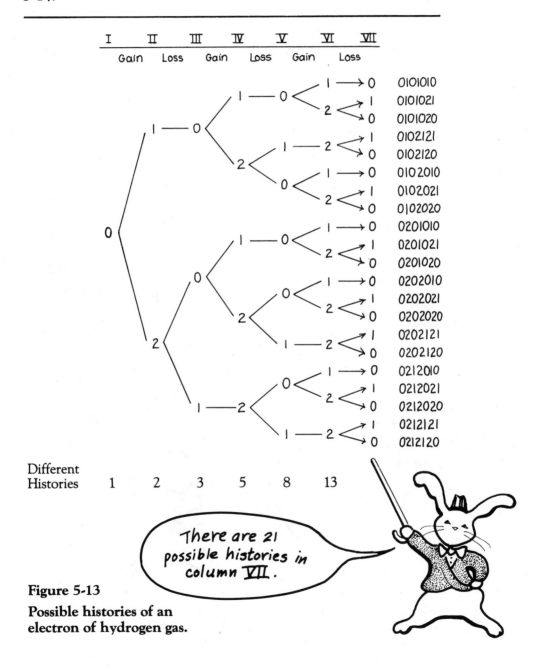

Figure 5-13

Possible histories of an electron of hydrogen gas.

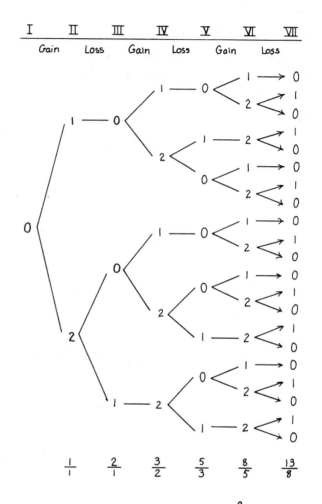

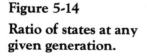

In column VI there are 8 state 2 energy levels and 5 state 1 energy levels. A FIBONACCI RATIO!

Figure 5-14

Ratio of states at any given generation.

There are many other scientific inquiries in which Fibonacci numbers figure prominently. Distinguished researchers claim to see Fibonacci relationships in the periodic table of elements used by chemists. Geneticists in Australia have used a Fibonacci-type formula in their studies of inbreeding in poultry. Astronomers have found that Fibonacci numbers operate in a formula used to predict the distances of the moons of Jupiter, Saturn, and Uranus (possibly Mars and Neptune as well) from their respective planets. Engineers have discovered that the Fibonacci sequence determines the alternation of long and short spacings along the axes of "quasicrystals," an area of exciting research in current solid-state physics.

Indeed, modern technology owes a considerable debt to the Fibonacci sequence. Because the series has useful applications in such tasks as sorting data, searching for information, and generating random numbers, it is used extensively in computer science. Beginning students in programming frequently get exposure to the Fibonacci sequence in exercises designed to teach the computer language BASIC. Here are five simple programs that generate the Fibonacci sequence—almost instantaneously.

```
10   X = 1
20   Z = X + Y: PRINT Z
30   X = Y: Y = Z: GOTO 20

10   X = 1
20   Y = X: X = Z
30   Z = X + Y: PRINT Z;" ";: GOTO 20

10   X = 1: Y = 1: PRINT 1;1;
20   Z = X + Y: PRINT Z,
30   X = Y: Y = Z: GOTO 20

10   Y = 1
20   PRINT Y: Z = X + Y
30   X = Y: Y = Z: GOTO 20

10   X = 1: Y = 1
20   PRINT X: ?" "; Y:?" ";
30   X = X + Y: Y = X + Y: GOTO 20
```

Following is another program in BASIC that will generate Fibonacci ratios. The output of this program reveals just how rapidly and accurately the Fibonacci ratios approximate the golden proportion (see figure 5-15).

```
10 LET A = 1
20 LET B = 1
30 LET C = A/B
40 PRINT C
50 LET D = A + B
60 LET A = B
70 LET B = D
80 GOTO 30
```

```
]RUN


1
.5
.666666667
.6
.625
.615384615
.619047619
.617647059
.618181818
.617977528
.618055556
.618025751
.618037135
.618032787
.618034448
.618033813
.618034056
.618033963
.618033998
.618033985
.61803399
.618033988
.618033989
.618033989
.618033989
.618033989
.618033989
.618033989
.618033989
.618033989
.618033989
.618033989
.618033989
.618033989
.618033989
.618033989
.618033989
```

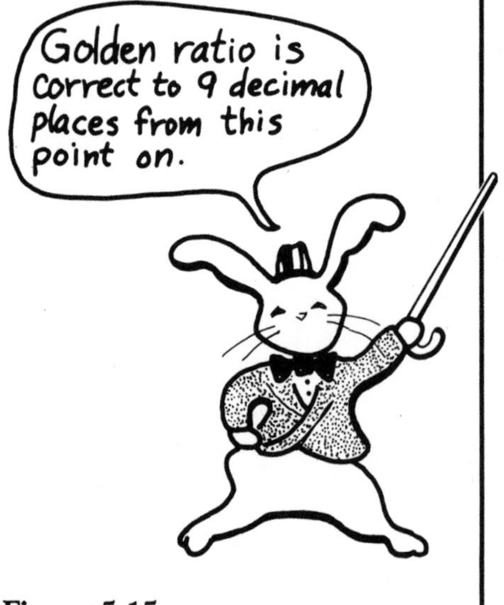
Golden ratio is correct to 9 decimal places from this point on.

Figure 5-15

Fibonacci ratios generated by BASIC program.

The following program in the computer language LOGO will draw a perfect golden spiral. The commands to the LOGO turtle are provided here, along with translations:

TO SPIRAL : SIZE   (means to make a spiral beginning with a given unit)

REPEAT 6 [FD : SIZE LT 15]   (means to go forward 1 unit and make a 15° left turn 6 times)

SPIRAL : SIZE ✳ 1.618   (means to repeat from the beginning, but make the new unit 1.618 times the previous one)

END

This program will fit well on a monitor if run

SPIRAL : 0.1

Figure 5-16 shows how the LOGO turtle dutifully responds, incorporating a growth factor equal to the golden proportion (1.618)

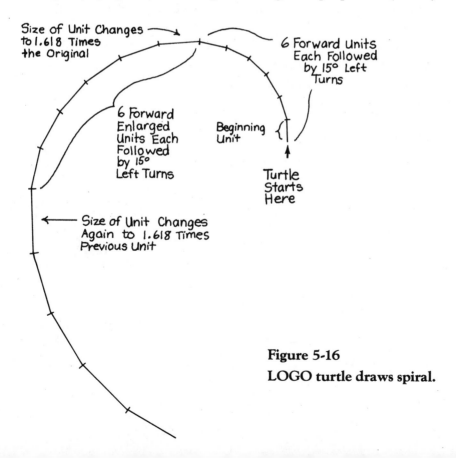

Size of Unit Changes to 1.618 Times the Original

6 Forward Units Each Followed by 15° Left Turns

6 Forward Enlarged Units Each Followed by 15° Left Turns

Beginning Unit

Turtle Starts Here

Size of Unit Changes Again to 1.618 Times Previous Unit

Figure 5-16
LOGO turtle draws spiral.

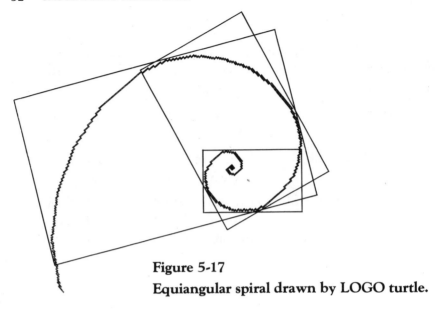

Figure 5-17
Equiangular spiral drawn by LOGO turtle.

after each quarter-circle turn. This assures that the beautiful resulting equiangular spiral will at all stages be characterized by Fibonacci proportions and will fit neatly into golden rectangles of increasing size, as shown in figure 5-17.

Perhaps nature has been using a similar factor for millions of years to create shells, claws, horns, beaks, ocean waves, and galaxies—to mention only a few of the many such spirals that occur naturally. In all these cases, the shape of the spiral remains the same while the size increases. This basic feat of engineering can now be simulated by a computer, but it has always been a characteristic of physical and biological growth.

CHAPTER 6

Fibonacci Numbers Abound

Fibonacci numbers, scattered liberally in unexpected places, tend to go unnoticed by all but the most discerning eye or the most inquisitive mind. Consider, for example, a hypothetical machine that sells tokens for games at a video arcade, an unlikely place to look for Fibonacci numbers. If such a machine dispenses any number of 25-cent tokens, but will accept as payment only quarters and half dollars—in exact amounts, one at a time—the following situation exists:

If one 25-cent token is purchased, there is only 1 way to pay for it	1 quarter	(q)
If two 25-cent tokens are purchased, there are 2 ways to pay	2 quarters 1 half dollar	(qq) (h)
If three 25-cent tokens are purchased, there are 3 ways to pay	3 quarters 1 half dollar and 1 quarter 1 quarter and 1 half dollar	(qqq) (hq) (qh)

Up to this point, it might seem that the number of ways of paying for tokens equals the number of tokens purchased. If, however, four tokens are purchased, there are 5 configurations of payment:

(qqqq)   (hh)   (qhq)   (hqq)   (qqh)

If five tokens are purchased, there are 8 configurations:

(hqqq)   (hhq)   (qhqq)   (qqqh)   (qqhq)   (hqh)   (qhh)
(qqqqq)

If six tokens are purchased, there are 13 configurations:

(qqqqqq)   (hhqq)   (hqhq)   (qhqh)   (qqqqh)   (qqqhq)
(qqhqq)   (qhqqq)   (hqqqq)   (hqqh)   (qhhq)   (qqhh)
(hhh)

If seven tokens are purchased, there are 21 different ways of paying for them:

(hhhq)   (hhqh)   (hqhh)   (qhhh)   (hhqqq)   (hqhqq)
(hqqhq)   (hqqqh)   (qhqqh)   (qqhqh)   (qqqhh)   (qqhhq)
(qhqhq)   (qhhqq)   (qqqqqqq)   (qqqqqh)   (qqqqhq)
(qqqhqq)   (qqhqqq)   (qhqqqq)   (hqqqqq)

This could be summarized as follows:

No. of Tokens Issued	No. of Configurations of Payment
1	1
2	2
3	3
4	5
5	8
6	13
7	21
.	.
.	.
.	.

Clearly, then, Fibonacci numbers could be useful in predicting the number of ways such a machine must be programmed to accept coins relative to the number of tokens it is prepared to issue at a time.

There are other examples of Fibonacci numbers operating where one would hardly expect to find them. Suppose it were necessary to determine the number of paths by which a bee could crawl to neighboring cells in a hive such as pictured in figure 6-1, assuming it always moves in one general direction (right) and never backtracks.

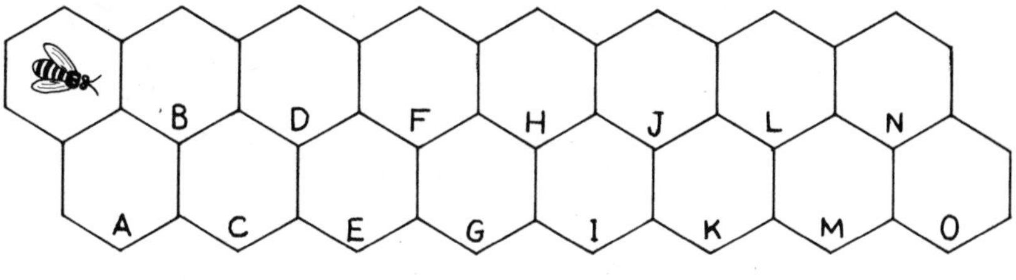

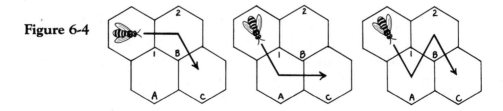

Figure 6-1

There is 1 path it could take to cell A (figure 6-2).

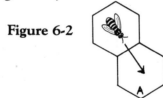

Figure 6-2

There are 2 paths it could take to cell B (figure 6-3).

Figure 6-3

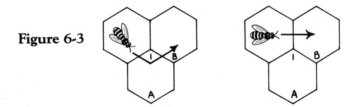

There are 3 paths it could take to cell C (figure 6-4).

Figure 6-4

There are 5 paths it could take to cell D (figure 6-5).

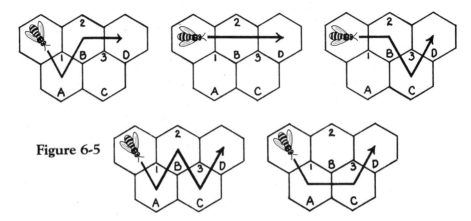

Figure 6-5

There are 8 paths it could take to cell E (figure 6-6).

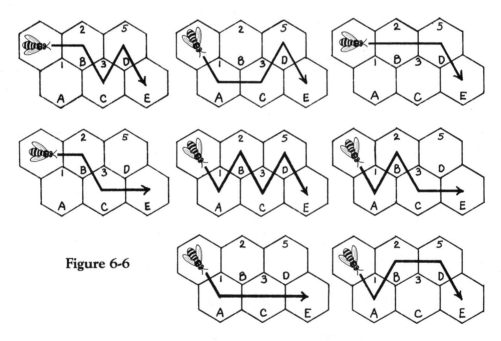

Figure 6-6

At some point, it becomes apparent that the number of paths to any given cell is the sum of the number of paths to the cells immediately preceding it. Since there are two cells immediately preceding each one, and the original numbers were 1 and 2, the number representing their sum will always be a Fibonacci number.

One of the most intriguing instances of the Fibonacci sequence at work is in the operation of the stock market. In the mid-1930s, as the country was emerging from the Great Depression, Ralph Nelson Elliot spent considerable time studying the history and movements of the Dow Jones industrial average. Noticing certain repetitions in the stock market's gyrations, he agreed with other observers that the market was not like a balloon plunging aimlessly hither and thither but that it tended to move in an orderly fashion. It is generally understood that upward and downward business swings are caused by rhythmic alterations of human optimism and pessimism. In a sense, business cycles are a function of human behavior, which tends to follow patterns; these patterns are ultimately reflected in the stock market.

Elliot's observations are summarized in the Elliot Wave Principle, one of the theories used in the investment industry today to predict turns in the stock market. Elliot noticed that the market unfolds according to a basic pattern of 5 waves generally up and 3 waves generally down, forming a complete cycle of 8 waves (see figure 6-7). The 5 upward waves (numbered phase) include 2 that are actually down, and the 3 downward waves (lettered phase) include 1 that is actually up. Upward waves are impulses (optimism), and downward waves are corrections of those impulses (pessimism). There are waves

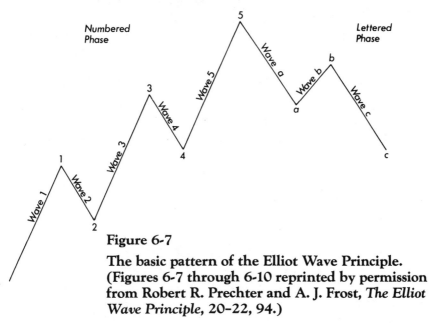

Figure 6-7

The basic pattern of the Elliot Wave Principle. (Figures 6-7 through 6-10 reprinted by permission from Robert R. Prechter and A. J. Frost, *The Elliot Wave Principle*, 20–22, 94.)

Figure 6-8

Waves within waves.

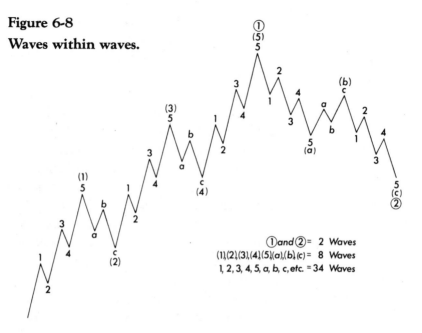

$\textcircled{1}$ and $\textcircled{2}$ = 2 Waves
(1),(2),(3),(4),(5),(a),(b),(c) = 8 Waves
1, 2, 3, 4, 5, a, b, c, etc. = 34 Waves

within waves, as shown in figure 6-8. Waves can be further subdivided or become parts of bigger waves, as shown in figure 6-9. Waves may become stretched or compressed and are subject to various irregularities and overriding trends, but the underlying pattern is constant.

An analysis of various wave densities reveals Fibonacci numbers at all stages (see figure 6-10). These patterns and the Fibonacci numbers they represent can continue indefinitely.

Figure 6-9

Waves as parts of bigger waves.

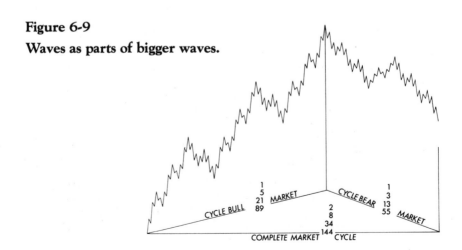

Figure 6-10
Fibonacci numbers at various wave densities.

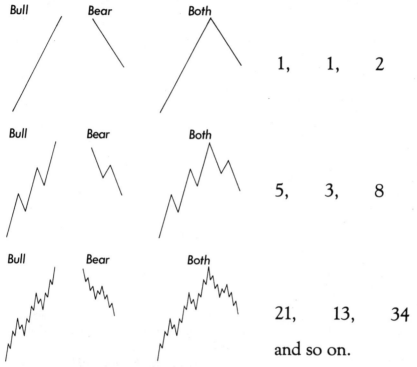

Bull   Bear   Both

1,   1,   2

Bull   Bear   Both

5,   3,   8

Bull   Bear   Both

21,   13,   34

and so on.

Elliot believed that the Fibonacci sequence was one of the keys to the operation of mass psychology. Today his followers include some distinguished stock market technicians, who use the Elliot Wave Principle in forecasting market trends.

Fibonacci proportions seem to exist in other areas of psychology as well. Researchers in Canada have concluded from their studies that people tend to view others positively or negatively in certain consistent proportions. Subjects were asked to characterize acquaintances with one or the other of two opposing attributes, such as generous (+)/stingy (−), pleasant (+)/unpleasant (−), fair (+)/unfair (−), strong (+)/weak (−), happy (+)/sad (−), and energetic (+)/lethargic (−). It was found that people attached positive attributes to others about 62 percent of the time and negative attributes about 38 percent of the time. For all practical purposes, this is the golden proportion.

Children (age 10) tend to be more positive in their assessment of others (70 percent positive), but adolescents (age 14) test as adults do.

Psychologists have pointed out that the positive member of a pair of opposite adjectives is usually the one that came into the language first, occurs more frequently, and is the first to be used correctly by children. Some studies indicate that people divide all things, not just acquaintances, into positives and negatives in a ratio of 0.618 to 0.382. All of this seems to suggest a general human emphasis on the positive, to which the Elliot Wave Principle also testifies.

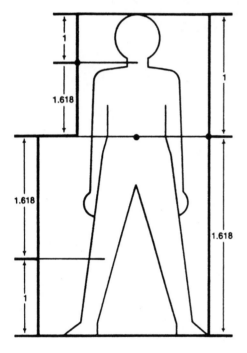

Figure 6-11

The Modular—Le Corbusier's study of human proportion. (Reprinted with permission from the 1977 Yearbook of Science and the Future, 191.)

The discovery that human thought and behavior are characterized by the golden proportion seems consistent with the fact that the human body divides nicely into those same proportions. Architect Le Corbusier designed a study of human proportions called The Modular, shown in figure 6-11, which he used in his work. It clearly demonstrates that the navel separates the entire body into golden proportions, the neck further divides the upper portion, and the knee divides the lower portion. Other golden proportions can also be seen. The head fits into a golden rectangle, and the face divides into Fibonaccian proportions (see figure 6-12), as does the hand (see figure 6-13). People all have their own personal golden rectangle available to them quite literally at their fingertips (see figure 6-14).

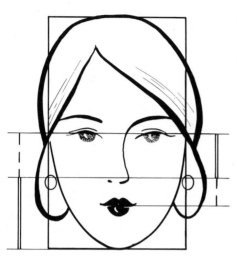

Figure 6-12

The golden proportions of the human head and face.

$$\frac{A}{B} = \frac{B}{A + B} \qquad \frac{A}{B} = \frac{B}{C}$$

$$\frac{B}{C} = \frac{C}{B + C} \qquad \frac{B}{C} = \frac{C}{D}$$

and so on.

Figure 6-13

The golden proportions of the human hand.

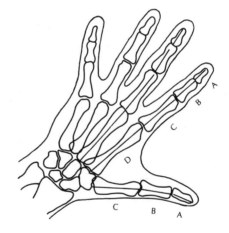

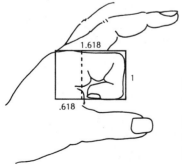

Figure 6-14

Your personal golden rectangle. (Figures 6-13 and 6-14 reprinted with permission from Bruce Haughey, *Dynamic Composition*, 26, 30.)

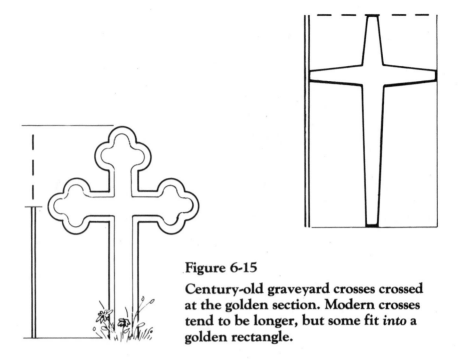

Figure 6-15

Century-old graveyard crosses crossed at the golden section. Modern crosses tend to be longer, but some fit *into* a golden rectangle.

There seems to be no end to the practical applications of the golden proportion, although its use is subject to the trends of time and fashion. For example, most graveyard crosses in Europe may have "crossed" at the golden section a century ago, but modern crosses more often do not. Today, many have a more streamlined look, although sometimes they will fit *into* a golden rectangle (see figure 6-15). Historically, the geometric proportions of letters of the alphabet were frequently golden, but today it would be difficult to make any such generalization about lettering; so many technologies are available now, and so many more factors enter into the art of printing, that the variety of letter types and proportions is enormous. Golden rectangles have been identified in ancient game boards; today game boards differ widely, although golden rectangles can clearly be seen in some, such as a modern Monopoly board (see figure 6-16). Stamps are often shaped in perfect golden rectangles, but they are also subject to variation, in this case depending on the whims of regional postal services.

Golden proportions seem to figure prominently in the art of violin making. The golden point (G) of the violin occurs at the intersection of two lines passing through the center of the f-holes as shown in figure 6-17. The body and neck are also in golden proportion. The strategic placement of bolts is often determined by the golden section, and the head of a violin approximates an equiangular spiral.

Some investigators have observed a relationship between the Fibonacci branching pattern and the way streams flow together into rivers—a sort of reverse branching. Fibonacci numbers have proven useful in predicting the growth of a city's energy needs and the most economical location of water pollution control plants.

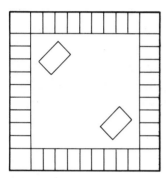

Figure 6-16

Golden rectangles on a game board.

Figure 6-17

Golden proportions in violin construction.

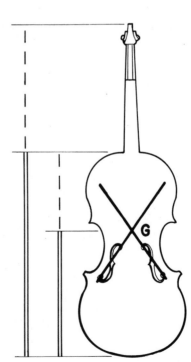

Figure 6-18

The eye sees a golden rectangle when a clock is set to 10:10.

One obscure but consistent "sighting" of the golden rectangle bears mentioning. Nondigital clocks and watches on display in stores or in advertisements are typically set at approximately 10:10 or 8:20 (see figure 6-18). Explanations for this range from "it looks good" to "there's room on the rest of the clock for advertising" to "that was the time when Abraham Lincoln died." One researcher has suggested, however, that this setting is visually pleasing because the eye tends to see on the face of the clock a portion of a golden rectangle, which it completes mentally.* Convincing trigonometric calculations support this theory.

---

*M. G. Monzingo, "Why Are 8:18 and 10:09 Such Pleasant Times?" (*Fibonacci Quarterly* 21 (May 1983).

CHAPTER 7

The Mathematics of Fibonacci Numbers

To the casual observer, Fibonacci numbers may appear to be nothing more than random numbers. Some are odd (13, 21), some are even (8, 34), some are prime (5, 89), some are composite (55, 144), and the distances between them vary. But the intuitive or informed eye will note the sequence we have described in so many contexts in this book: each Fibonacci number is the sum of the previous two numbers, beginning with 1.

$$0+1 \quad 1+1 \quad 1+2 \quad 2+3 \quad 3+5 \quad 5+8$$

$$1, \ 1, \ 2, \ 3, \ 5, \ 8, \ 13, \ \ldots$$

The simplest of all numbers is, of course, 1. By following it with another 1 (the sum of the first 1 and the zero that precedes it), we can generate an infinite sequence of numbers. Any two adjacent numbers create the next number by addition.

The Fibonacci squence is called a *recursive* sequence because each number is a function of the preceding two numbers, both of which change as the sequence progresses. This is in contrast to other sequences:

1. In an arithmetic sequence, each number is the sum of a specific number and the previous number—for example,
    1, 4, 7, 10, 13, . . .   (+ 3 each time).

2. In a geometric sequence each number is the product of a specific number and the previous number—for example,
    1, 3, 9, 27, 81, . . .   (× 3 each time).

3. In a power sequence each number is a specific power of a sequential number—for example,
    1, 4, 9, 16, 25, . . .   (2nd power of counting numbers).

Another closely related recursive sequence is the Lucas sequence. It begins with 1 and 3, and from that point on each number is the sum of the previous two:

$$1+3 \quad 3+4 \quad 4+7 \quad 7+11 \quad 11+18$$

$$1, \ 3, \ 4, \ 7, \ 11, \ 18, \ 29, \ . \ . \ .$$

The first 12 Lucas numbers are 1, 3, 4, 7, 11, 18, 29, 47, 76, 123, 199, 322. Lucas numbers also appear in nature, frequently as deviations from the more usual Fibonacci numbers (occasional phyllotactic ratios and sunflower spirals, for example). Lucas ratios also produce the golden proportion, although comparable proportions require larger Lucas numbers than Fibonacci numbers.

The mathematical properties of Fibonacci numbers are fascinating. The following are just a few examples selected from an enormous amount of literature on the subject.

1. No two consecutive Fibonacci numbers have any common factors.

Number	Prime Factorization
1	—
1	—
2	2
3	3
5	5
8	$2 \times 2 \times 2$
13	13
21	3×7
34	2×17
55	5×11
89	89
144	$2 \times 2 \times 2 \times 2 \times 3 \times 3$
233	233
377	13×29
610	$2 \times 5 \times 61$

no like factors in adjacent numbers!

---

2. The twelfth Fibonacci number is the square of 12. A mathematician at the University of London proved in 1963 that 144 is the only square number in the entire infinite sequence (except 1). The only cubic number is 8.

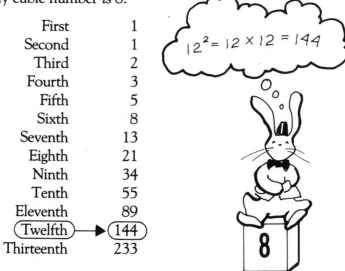

First	1
Second	1
Third	2
Fourth	3
Fifth	5
Sixth	8
Seventh	13
Eighth	21
Ninth	34
Tenth	55
Eleventh	89
Twelfth →	144
Thirteenth	233

$12^2 = 12 \times 12 = 144$

3. The sum of any ten consecutive Fibonacci numbers is always evenly divisible by 11.

1	5
1	8
2	13
3	21
5	34
8	55
13	89
21	144
34	233
+ 55	+ 377
143 / 11 = 13	979 / 11 = 89

89
144
233
377
610
987
1,597
2,584
4,181
+ 6,765
17,567 / 11 = 1,597

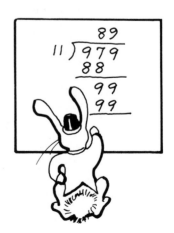

4. Every 3rd Fibonacci number is divisible by 2.
Every 4th Fibonacci number is divisible by 3.
Every 5th Fibonacci number is divisible by 5.
Every 6th Fibonacci number is divisible by 8.
Every 7th Fibonacci number is divisible by 13.
Every 8th Fibonacci number is divisible by 21.
Etc.

Consecutive Integers

Consecutive Fibonacci Numbers

5. The eleventh Fibonacci number (89) is singularly remarkable. Its reciprocal, 1/89, can be generated by adding the Fibonacci sequence . . . very carefully!

Begin writing Fibonacci numbers.

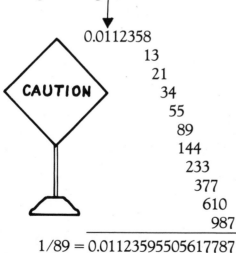

```
0.0112358
        13
        21
        34
        55
        89
       144
       233
       377
       610
       987
```

CAUTION

$1/89 = 0.01123595505617787$

Each Fibonacci number contributes 1 decimal digit to this enormous repeating decimal, with tens, hundreds, and so on, being added under preceding digits.

Etc.

6. Twice any Fibonacci number minus the next Fibonacci number equals the second number preceding the original one.

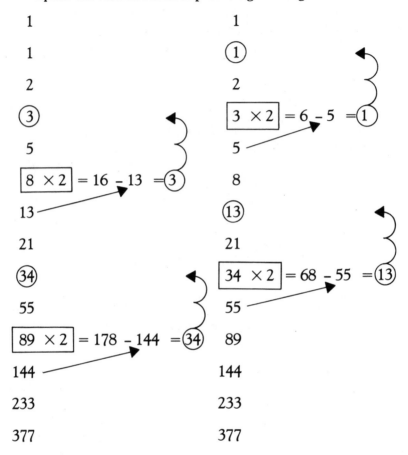

$$\begin{array}{r} 233 \\ \times\ 2 \\ \hline 466 \\ -\ 377 \\ \hline 89 \end{array}$$

7. The product of any two alternating Fibonacci numbers differs from the square of the middle number by 1.

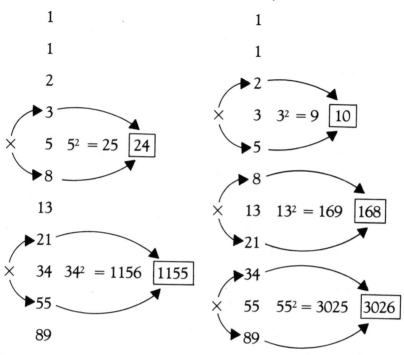

$$1$$
$$1$$
$$2$$
$$3$$
$$\times \quad 5 \quad 5^2 = 25 \quad \boxed{24}$$
$$8$$
$$13$$
$$\times \quad 21$$
$$34 \quad 34^2 = 1156 \quad \boxed{1155}$$
$$55$$
$$89$$

$$1$$
$$1$$
$$2$$
$$\times \quad 3 \quad 3^2 = 9 \quad \boxed{10}$$
$$5$$
$$8$$
$$\times \quad 13 \quad 13^2 = 169 \quad \boxed{168}$$
$$21$$
$$34$$
$$\times \quad 55 \quad 55^2 = 3025 \quad \boxed{3026}$$
$$89$$

8. If Fibonacci numbers are squared and the adjacent squares are added together, a sequence of alternate Fibonacci numbers emerges.

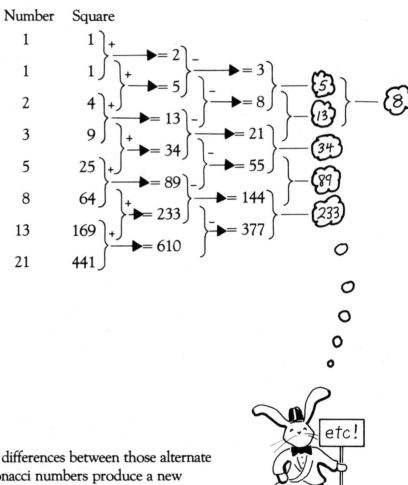

Number	Square
1	1
1	1
2	4
3	9
5	25
8	64
13	169
21	441

= 2
= 5
= 13
= 34
= 89
= 233
= 610

= 3
= 8
= 21
= 55
= 144
= 377

5
13
34
89
233

8

etc!

The differences between those alternate Fibonacci numbers produce a new sequence of alternate Fibonacci numbers.

9. The difference of the squares of alternate Fibonacci numbers is always a Fibonacci number.

Number	Square			Number	Square	
1	1			1	1	
1	①⎫			1	1	
2	4⎬──→8			2	④⎫	
3	⑨⎭			3	9⎬──→21	
5	㉕⎫			5	㉕⎭	
8	64⎬──→144			8	㉔⎫	
13	⑯⑨⎭			13	169⎬──→377	
21	④④①⎫			21	④④①⎭	
34	1,156⎬──→2,584			34	1,156⎫	
55	③,⓪②⑤⎭			55	3,025⎬──→6,765	
89	7,921			89	⑦,⑨②①⎭	
144	20,736			144	20,736	
233	54,289			233	54,289	

$$54,289$$
$$-\ \ 7,921$$
$$\overline{46,368}\ !$$

10. For any four consecutive Fibonacci numbers, the difference of the squares of the middle two numbers equals the product of the smallest and largest numbers.

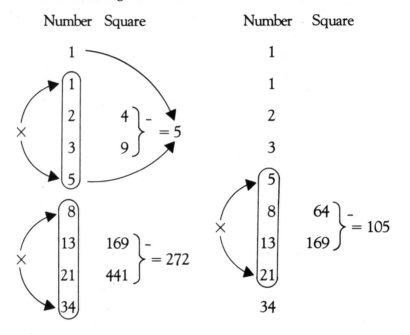

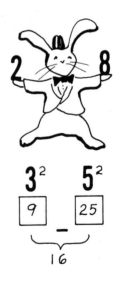

3^2 5^2

9 25

$-$

16

11. The squares of Fibonacci numbers add up as follows:

$$1^2 + 1^2 = 1 \times 2$$

$$1^2 + 1^2 + 2^2 = 2 \times 3$$

...next Fibonacci number

$$1^2 + 1^2 + 2^2 + 3^2 = 3 \times 5$$

$$1^2 + 1^2 + 2^2 + 3^2 + 5^2 = 5 \times 8$$

$$1^2 + 1^2 + 2^2 + 3^2 + 5^2 + 8^2 = 8 \times 13$$

$$1^2 + 1^2 + 2^2 + 3^2 + 5^2 + 8^2 + 13^2 = 13 \times 21$$

$$1^2 + 1^2 + 2^2 + 3^2 + 5^2 + 8^2 + 13^2 + 21^2 = 21 \times 34 \qquad \text{etc.}$$

---

12. For any three Fibonacci numbers, the sum of the cubes of the two greatest minus the cube of the smallest equals a Fibonacci number.

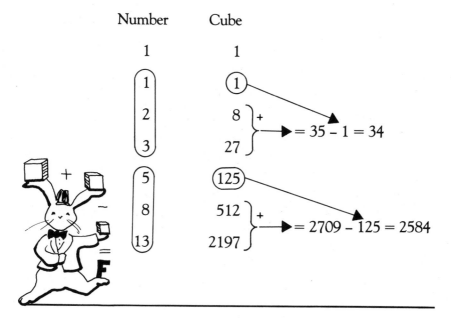

Number	Cube
1	1
1	1
2	8
3	27

$$= 35 - 1 = 34$$

5	125
8	512
13	2197

$$= 2709 - 125 = 2584$$

13. The Fibonacci numbers can be found in Pascal's triangle, one of the most famous of all number patterns. At the apex of Pascal's triangle is 1. The row below it consists of two more 1's, placed on either side of the original 1. The numbers in subsequent rows are each the sum of the two numbers immediately above them.

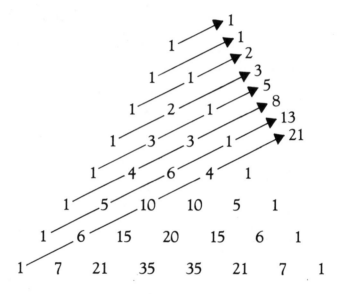

If diagonals are drawn beginning at each 1 along the left-hand side (passing under the 1 just above) and extending to the far side of the triangle, the numbers they pass through add up to sequential Fibonacci numbers. There is no record that Pascal (a seventeenth-century mathematician) ever noticed this, but Fibonacci might have—while examining a Chinese triangle that is known to have existed in his time. A Chinese triangle is a Pascal's triangle with the 1's on the left-hand side vertically aligned.

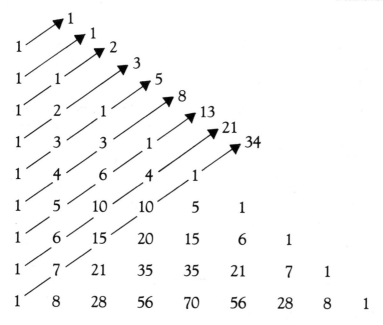

Fibonacci numbers are a little easier to spot in the Chinese triangle, since they lie on true diagonals.

14. The sum of any number of Fibonacci numbers beginning with the first 1 is always equal to 1 less than the second number beyond the last one added. This is a convenient fact to know when you are playing the "lightning addition trick"—you appear to be able to add *very* fast.

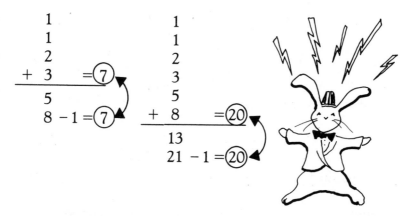

15. Although much more is known about the mathematical properties of Fibonacci numbers than what is mentioned here, there
remains one *great Fibonacci mystery:*

Is there one greatest Fibonacci prime
number, or is there an infinite number
of prime Fibonacci numbers?

The largest known Fibonacci prime is the 2971st number in the
sequence. What is not known is whether there are any more,
and if so, how many.

The relationship between Fibonacci ratios and the golden ratio is
a curious phenomenon, as mentioned in chapter 3, and it has been the
subject of study and speculation for generations. The golden ratio
(0.618034 . . .), to which Fibonacci ratios get increasingly close, is an
irrational number that can be accurately expressed only using a square
root. (Although decimal and fraction approximations are sufficient for
practical purposes, they are truly only approximations.)

The exact equivalent of the golden ratio can be derived by using
the definition of the golden section and some elementary algebra:

The golden "cut" on this line segment is that point at which the
ratio of the small is to the large as the large is to the whole. If x is the
small, unknown segment and 1 is the large one, the ratio is expressed
mathematically as follows:

$$\frac{x}{1} = \frac{1}{x + 1}$$

Cross products are equal: $x(x + 1) = 1$

Multiply: $x^2 + x = 1$ (quadratic equation)

Set equal to 0: $x^2 + x - 1 = 0$

Solve:
(Use quadratic formula
where for $ax^2 + bx + c = 0$

$x = \dfrac{-b \pm \sqrt{b^2 - 4ac}}{2a}$

and $a = 1$, $b = 1$, and $c = -1$)

$x = \dfrac{-1 \pm \sqrt{1 - [4 \times 1 \times (-1)]}}{2 \times 1}$

$x = \dfrac{-1 \pm \sqrt{1 + 4}}{2}$

$x = \dfrac{-1 \pm \sqrt{5}}{2}$

The negative root is meaningless in this problem since x is a positive distance, but the positive root is the exact equivalent of the small portion of the original segment. To avoid a leading negative, that ratio is often expressed

$$\dfrac{\sqrt{5} - 1}{2}$$

Substituting the decimal approximation of $\sqrt{5}$, which is 2.236, we get

$$\dfrac{2.236 - 1}{2} = \dfrac{1.236}{2} = 0.618!$$

The construction of the golden rectangle is a simple exercise in elementary geometry, as explained below.

Begin with a square *ABCD*, as shown in figure 7-1.

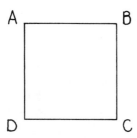

Figure 7-1

Let *E* be the midpoint of side *DC*. Using *E* as the center and *EB* as the radius, construct a quarter-circle arc that intersects extended side *DC* at point *F*, as shown in figure 7-2.

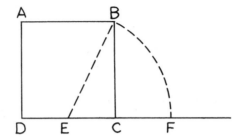

Figure 7-2

Construct a line perpendicular to *DF* at *F*. Extend *AB* to intersect that perpendicular line, as shown in figure 7-3.

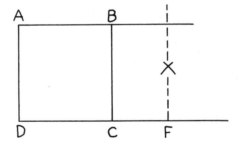

Figure 7-3

What emerges is a perfect golden rectangle, as shown in figure 7-4.

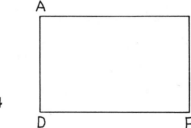

Figure 7-4

If three identical golden rectangles intersect each other symmetrically, each perpendicular to the other two, the corners of the rectangles will mark the 12 corners of a regular icosahedron (a 20-sided figure, each side being an equiangular triangle). The corners will also coincide with the centers of the sides of a dodecahedron (a 12-sided figure, each side being a regular pentagon). Figure 7-5 shows both of these figures.

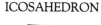
ICOSAHEDRON

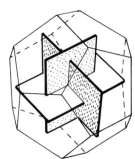
DODECAHEDRON

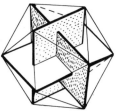

Figure 7-5

Golden rectangles define an icosahedron, on the left, and a dodecahedron, on the right.

This geometric curiosity can be verified by examining the figure formed by the intersection of three index cards (of Fibonacci proportions) cut along the patterns shown in figure 7-6.

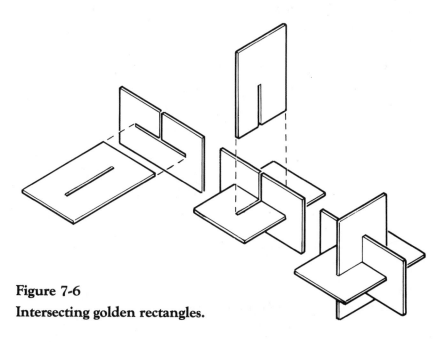

Figure 7-6

Intersecting golden rectangles.

Figure 7-7
Golden triangles.

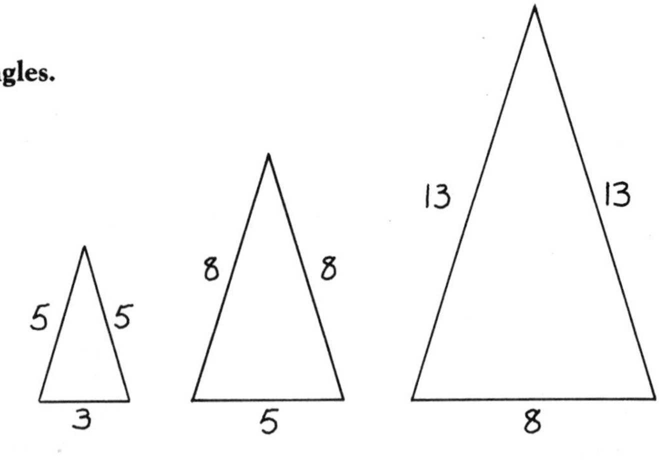

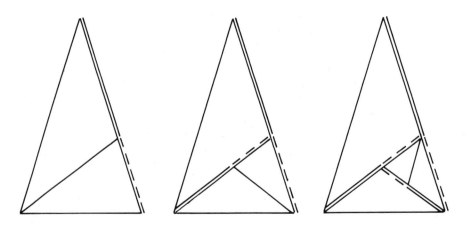

In addition to the golden rectangle, there is also a golden triangle. It is an isosceles triangle with one short side in golden proportion to each of the two longer, equal sides. Fibonacci numbers can be used to construct such triangles, as shown in figure 7-7. Among the interesting properties of the golden triangle is the fact that the bisector of a base angle (which is always 72°) cuts the side opposite it into the golden proportions. That bisector also cuts the triangle into two new isosceles triangles (one of which is the same shape as the original triangle) whose areas are in golden proportion to each other. The process can be

Figure 7-8
Golden triangles, showing proportions.

repeated endlessly, as shown in figure 7-8. An equiangular spiral can be constructed around the golden triangle as well as the golden rectangle, as shown in figure 7-9.

Figure 7-9

Golden spiral constructed with golden triangles.

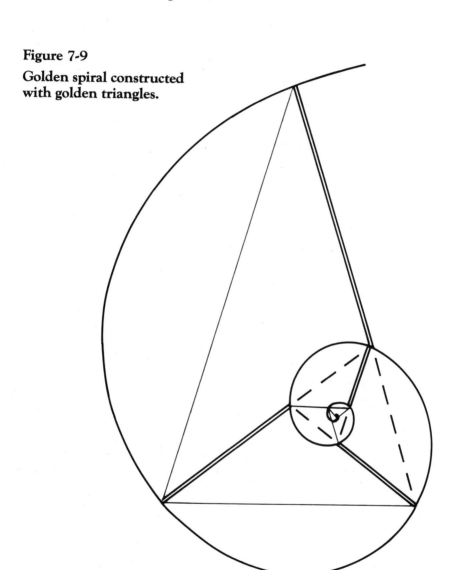

There is more intriguing geometry associated with the Fibonacci numbers. Consider the following paradox, which Lewis Carroll, the author of *Alice in Wonderland*, liked to ask his friends to solve:

> Take a square 8 units on a side. Cut it into sections as shown in figure 7-10. Then reposition the sections as shown in figure 7-11. The area of the square is 64, but the area of the rectangle is 65! The same thing will happen with any Fibonacci square (see figure 7-12). How can this be? (The answer is at the end of this chapter.)

Figure 7-10   **Figure 7-11**

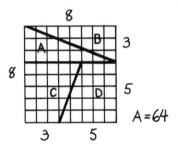

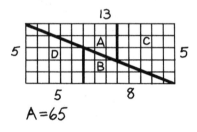

Figure 7-12

Compare the areas of the squares and rectangles. Where is the missing unit?

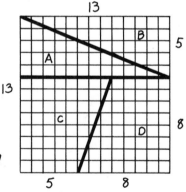

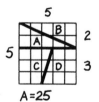

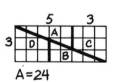

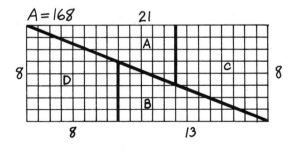

The Fibonacci sequence is a virtual Pandora's box of curiosities and intrigue that scholars and mathematicians have been exploring for decades. A list of the first 100 Fibonacci numbers and their prime factorizations is given in table 7-1. A list of the first 50 Lucas numbers and their prime factorizations is given in table 7-2. Surely there are some relationships and puzzles yet to be discovered here.

Table 7-1 Fibonacci Numbers and Their Prime Factorizations

n	F_n	Factors of F_n
1	1	
2	1	
3	2	**2***
4	3	**3**
5	5	**5**
6	8	2^3
7	13	**13**
8	21	$3 \cdot$ **7**
9	34	$2 \cdot$ **17**
10	55	$5 \cdot$ **11**
11	89	**89**
12	144	$2^4 \cdot 3^2$
13	233	**233**
14	377	$13 \cdot$ **29**
15	610	$2 \cdot 5 \cdot$ **61**
16	987	$3 \cdot 7 \cdot$ **47**
17	1597	**1597**
18	2584	$2^3 \cdot 17 \cdot$ **19**
19	4181	**37** $\cdot$ **113**
20	6765	$3 \cdot 5 \cdot 11 \cdot$ **41**
21	10946	$2 \cdot 13 \cdot$ **421**
22	17711	$89 \cdot$ **199**
23	28657	**28657**
24	46368	$2^5 \cdot 3^2 \cdot 7 \cdot$ **23**
25	75025	$5^2 \cdot$ **3001**
26	121393	$233 \cdot$ **521**
27	196418	$2 \cdot 17 \cdot$ **53** $\cdot$ **109**
28	317811	$2 \cdot 13 \cdot 29 \cdot$ **281**
29	514229	**514229**

(continued on next page)

Source: Brother U. Alfred Brousseau, *An Introduction to Fibonacci Discovery* (San Jose, CA: San Jose State University, The Fibonacci Association, 1965), 52. Reprinted with permission.
***Bold type** indicates a factor's first appearance in the list.

Table 7-1 continued

n	F_n	Factors of F_n
30	832040	$2^3 \cdot 5 \cdot 11 \cdot 31 \cdot 61$
31	1346269	**577 · 2417**
32	2178309	$3 \cdot 7 \cdot 47 \cdot \mathbf{2207}$
33	3524578	$2 \cdot 89 \cdot \mathbf{19801}$
34	5702887	1597 · **3571**
35	9227465	$5 \cdot 13 \cdot \mathbf{141961}$
36	14930352	$2^4 \cdot 3^3 \cdot 17 \cdot 19 \cdot \mathbf{107}$
37	24157817	**73 · 149 · 2221**
38	39088169	37 · 113 · **9349**
39	63245986	$2 \cdot 233 \cdot \mathbf{135721}$
40	102334155	$3 \cdot 5 \cdot 7 \cdot 11 \cdot 41 \cdot \mathbf{2161}$
41	165580141	**2789 · 59369**
42	267914296	$2^3 \cdot 13 \cdot 29 \cdot \mathbf{211} \cdot \mathbf{421}$
43	433494437	**433494437**
44	701408733	$3 \cdot \mathbf{43} \cdot 89 \cdot \mathbf{199} \cdot \mathbf{307}$
45	1134903170	$2 \cdot 5 \cdot 17 \cdot 61 \cdot \mathbf{109441}$
46	1836311903	**139 · 461 · 28657**
47	2971215073	**2971215073**
48	4807526976	$2^6 \cdot 3^2 \cdot 7 \cdot 23 \cdot 47 \cdot \mathbf{1103}$
49	7778742049	13 · **97 · 6168709**
50	12586269025	$5^2 \cdot 11 \cdot 101 \cdot 151 \cdot \mathbf{3001}$
51	20365011074	2 · 1597 · **6376021**
52	32951280099	$3 \cdot 233 \cdot \mathbf{521} \cdot \mathbf{90481}$
53	53316291173	**953 · 55945741**
54	86267571272	$2^3 \cdot 17 \cdot 19 \cdot 53 \cdot \mathbf{109} \cdot \mathbf{5779}$
55	139583862445	$5 \cdot 89 \cdot \mathbf{661} \cdot \mathbf{474541}$
56	225851433717	$3 \cdot 7 \cdot 7 \cdot 13 \cdot 29 \cdot \mathbf{281} \cdot \mathbf{14503}$
57	365435296162	$2 \cdot 37 \cdot 113 \cdot \mathbf{797} \cdot \mathbf{54833}$
58	591286729879	**59 · 19489 · 514229**
59	956722026041	**353 · 2710260697**
60	1548008755920	$2^4 \cdot 3^2 \cdot 5 \cdot 11 \cdot 31 \cdot 41 \cdot 61 \cdot \mathbf{2521}$
61	2504730781961	**4513 · 555003497**
62	4052739537881	557 · 2417 · **3010349**
63	6557470319842	$2 \cdot 13 \cdot 17 \cdot 421 \cdot \mathbf{35239681}$
64	10610209857723	$3 \cdot 7 \cdot 47 \cdot \mathbf{1087} \cdot 2207 \cdot \mathbf{4481}$
65	17167680177565	$5 \cdot 233 \cdot \mathbf{14736206161}$
66	27777890035288	$2^3 \cdot 89 \cdot 199 \cdot \mathbf{9901} \cdot 19801$
67	44945570212853	**269 · 116849 · 1429913**
68	72723460248141	$3 \cdot \mathbf{67} \cdot 1597 \cdot 3571 \cdot \mathbf{63443}$
69	117669030460994	$2 \cdot \mathbf{137} \cdot \mathbf{829} \cdot \mathbf{18077} \cdot 28657$
70	190392490709135	$5 \cdot 11 \cdot 13 \cdot 29 \cdot 71 \cdot \mathbf{911} \cdot 141961$
71	308061521170129	**6673 · 46165371073**
72	498454011879264	$2^5 \cdot 3^3 \cdot 7 \cdot 17 \cdot 19 \cdot 23 \cdot 107 \cdot \mathbf{103681}$

(continued on next page)

Table 7-1 continued

n	F_n	Factors of F_n
73	806515533049393	$9375829 \cdot 86020717$
74	1304969544928657	$73 \cdot 149 \cdot 2221 \cdot 54018521$
75	2111485077978050	$2 \cdot 5^2 \cdot 61 \cdot 3001 \cdot 230686501$
76	3416454622906707	$3 \cdot 37 \cdot 113 \cdot 9349 \cdot 29134601$
77	5527939700884757	$13 \cdot 89 \cdot 988681 \cdot 4832521$
78	8944394323791464	$2^3 \cdot 79 \cdot 233 \cdot 521 \cdot 859 \cdot 135721$
79	14472334024676221	$157 \cdot 92180471494753$
80	23416728348467685	$3 \cdot 5 \cdot 7 \cdot 11 \cdot 41 \cdot 47 \cdot 1601 \cdot 2161 \cdot 3041$
81	37889062373143906	$2 \cdot 17 \cdot 53 \cdot 109 \cdot 2269 \cdot 4373 \cdot 19441$
82	61305790721611591	$2789 \cdot 59369 \cdot 370248451$
83	99194853094755497	99194853094755497
84	160500643816367088	$2^4 \cdot 3^2 \cdot 13 \cdot 29 \cdot 83 \cdot 211 \cdot 281 \cdot 421 \cdot 1427$
85	259695496911122585	$5 \cdot 1597 \cdot 9521 \cdot 3415914041$
86	420196140727489673	$6709 \cdot 144481 \cdot 433494437$
87	679891637638612258	$2 \cdot 173 \cdot 514229 \cdot 3821263937$
88	1100087778366101931	$3 \cdot 7 \cdot 43 \cdot 89 \cdot 199 \cdot 263 \cdot 307 \cdot 881 \cdot 967$
89	1779979416004714189	$1069 \cdot 1665088321800481$
90	2880067194370816120	$2^3 \cdot 5 \cdot 11 \cdot 17 \cdot 19 \cdot 31 \cdot 61 \cdot 181 \cdot 541 \cdot 109441$
91	4660046610375530309	$13 \cdot 13 \cdot 233 \cdot 741469 \cdot 159607993$
92	7540113804746346429	$3 \cdot 139 \cdot 461 \cdot 4969 \cdot 28657 \cdot 275449$
93	12200160415121876738	$2 \cdot 557 \cdot 2417 \cdot 4531100550901$
94	19740274219868223167	$2971215073 \cdot 6643838879$
95	31940434634990099905	$5 \cdot 37 \cdot 113 \cdot 761 \cdot 29641 \cdot 67735001$
96	51680708854858323072	$2^7 \cdot 3^2 \cdot 7 \cdot 23 \cdot 47 \cdot 769 \cdot 1103 \cdot 2207 \cdot 3167$
97	83621143489848422977	$193 \cdot 389 \cdot 3084989 \cdot 361040209$
98	135301852344706746049	$13 \cdot 29 \cdot 97 \cdot 6168709 \cdot 599786069$
99	218922995834555169026	$2 \cdot 17 \cdot 89 \cdot 197 \cdot 19801 \cdot 18546805133$
100	354224848179261915075	$3 \cdot 5^2 \cdot 11 \cdot 41 \cdot 101 \cdot 151 \cdot 401 \cdot 3001 \cdot 570601$

Table 7-2 Lucas Numbers and Their Prime Factorizations

n	L_n	Factors of L_n
1	1	
2	3	3
3	4	2^2
4	7	7
5	11	11
6	18	$2 \cdot 3^2$
7	29	29

(continued on next page)

Source: Brother U. Alfred Brousseau, *An Introduction to Fibonacci Discovery* (San Jose, CA: San Jose State University, The Fibonacci Association, 1965), 55. Reprinted with permission.

Table 7-2 continued

n	L_n	Factors of L_n
8	47	47
9	76	$2^2 \cdot 19$
10	123	$3 \cdot 41$
11	199	199
12	322	$2 \cdot 7 \cdot 23$
13	521	521
14	843	$3 \cdot 281$
15	1364	$2^2 \cdot 11 \cdot 31$
16	2207	2207
17	3571	3571
18	5778	$2 \cdot 3^3 \cdot 107$
19	9349	9349
20	15127	$7 \cdot 2161$
21	24476	$2^2 \cdot 29 \cdot 211$
22	39603	$3 \cdot 43 \cdot 307$
23	64079	$139 \cdot 461$
24	103682	$2 \cdot 47 \cdot 1103$
25	167761	$11 \cdot 101 \cdot 151$
26	271443	$3 \cdot 90481$
27	439204	$2^2 \cdot 19 \cdot 5779$
28	710647	$7^2 \cdot 14503$
29	1149851	$59 \cdot 19489$
30	1860498	$2 \cdot 3^2 \cdot 41 \cdot 2521$
31	3010349	3010349
32	4870847	$1087 \cdot 4481$
33	7881196	$2^2 \cdot 199 \cdot 9901$
34	12752043	$3 \cdot 67 \cdot 63443$
35	20633239	$11 \cdot 29 \cdot 71 \cdot 911$
36	33385282	$2 \cdot 7 \cdot 23 \cdot 103681$
37	54018521	54018521
38	87403803	$3 \cdot 29134601$
39	141422324	$2^2 \cdot 79 \cdot 521 \cdot 859$
40	228826127	$47 \cdot 1601 \cdot 3041$
41	370248451	370248451
42	599074578	$2 \cdot 3^2 \cdot 83 \cdot 281 \cdot 1427$
43	969323029	$6709 \cdot 144481$
44	1568397607	$7 \cdot 263 \cdot 881 \cdot 967$
45	2537720636	$2^2 \cdot 11 \cdot 19 \cdot 31 \cdot 181 \cdot 541$
46	4106118243	$3 \cdot 4969 \cdot 275449$
47	6643838879	6643838879
48	10749957122	$2 \cdot 769 \cdot 2207 \cdot 3167$
49	17393796001	$29 \cdot 599786069$
50	28143753123	$3 \cdot 41 \cdot 401 \cdot 570601$

Answer to Fibonacci Paradox

Although this problem *appears* to create a paradox, in fact it does not. If the pieces were cut out accurately and repositioned, there would be either a little overlap or a little space in the middle that would be equivalent to exactly 1 unit (see figure 7-13). The diagonals do not really line up accurately. The paradox is related to the relationship described earlier in this chapter in example number 7: the square of a Fibonacci number differs from the product of the numbers on either side of it by 1.

Figure 7-13
Where the missing unit is.

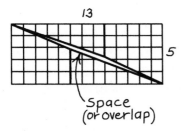

CHAPTER 8

Historical Perspective

"Divine proportions" have been around for a long time—at least 400 million years. Geologists and petroleum engineers in search of oil use fossilized remains of sea animals to date stratified layers of earth. Some animals, especially those related to the sponge, starfish, and chambered nautilus, exhibit Fibonacci characteristics and date back far into the Paleozoic era.

There is reason to believe that throughout early history many thinkers and scholars pondered the golden proportion and the numbers that generate it. The earliest documentation of a special ratio is found in the Rhind papyrus, a mathematical handbook discovered in Egypt in the mid-nineteenth century, dated 1600 BC. It refers to a "sacred ratio" in connection with the building of the pyramids of Egypt 1,000 years earlier. One can only speculate on how pervasive that ratio was in ancient architecture; little remains of it except the pyramids, which reveal extensive use of the golden proportion.

History records that Greek philosophers, mathematicians, and artists concerned themselves with various aspects of the golden proportion between the sixth and third centuries BC. Plato is reported to have considered it the "most binding of all mathematical relations, the key to the physics of the cosmos." Euclid solved the problem of finding the golden cut of a line in the second book of his *Elements*. Both he and Pythagoras referred to the "rectangle of the Divine Section." Pythagoras was the first to suspect that the proportion was the basis of the human figure, and he proved it to be so. Legend has it that the mathematician Eudoxos asked his friends to divide a stick into the proportions they found to be most pleasing and interesting—much as the psychologist Fechner did 2,100 years later in Germany.

The first person to record permanently specific numbers that generate the golden proportion was Leonardo of Pisa, as mentioned in chapter 1. He published his *Liber Abaci*, with its well-known rabbit problem, in 1202. Although he is variously known as Leonardo Pisano and Leonardo da Pisa, he usually wrote under the nickname Fibonacci (understood to be a contraction of *filius Bonacci*, Latin for "son of Bonacci"), by which he is commonly known today.

Leonardo was born in Pisa, Italy, in about 1175, at approximately the same time that construction began on the famous Leaning Tower in that city. As a young boy he moved to the north coast of Africa with his father, Bonacci, who worked as a customs official in a warehouse maintained by Pisan merchants in Bougie, Algeria.

There he is believed to have been educated by Muslim schoolmasters who taught him Hindu-Arabic numerals, the familiar 0, 1, 2, 3, 4, 5, 6, 7, 8, and 9. He recognized the superiority of these numerals over the clumsy Roman numerals in use at the time, I, V, X, L, C, D, and M. Calculating with Roman numerals required the use of an abacus, a flat device on which beads were moved in rows (see figure 8-1). But the

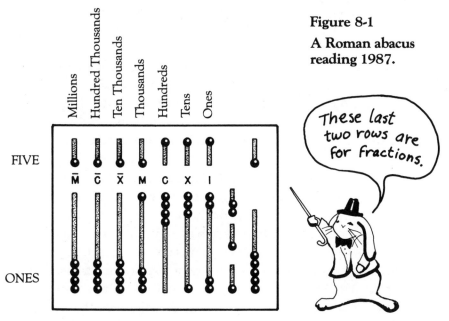

Figure 8-1

A Roman abacus reading 1987.

These last two rows are for fractions.

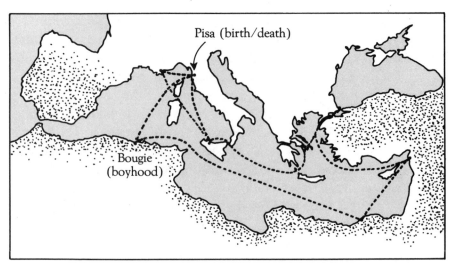

Figure 8-2

**Mediterranean Sea c. 1200,
showing the travels of
Fibonacci in his youth.**

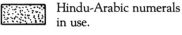

Hindu-Arabic numerals
in use.

Roman numerals in use.

columns used in calculating with Hindu-Arabic numerals function as
something of a built-in abacus. The availability of a zero to hold a place
where nothing else existed was unique; Leonardo was the first
Westerner to recognize its importance in a sophisticated numeration
system.

In the company of other merchants with whom the family
associated, Leonardo had the opportunity to travel extensively
throughout the Mediterranean in his youth. He visited Egypt, Syria,
Greece, Constantinople, Sicily, and southern France and was able to
compare the various methods of calculating used by the merchants in
those places (see figure 8-2). He became increasingly convinced of the
merits of the Hindu-Arabic numerals and system of calculating.

Returning to Pisa as a young man early in the thirteenth century,
Leonardo put into writing the mathematics he had acquired in his
travels. His book *Liber Abaci* was published in 1202, though hardly in
the style of "best sellers" today; his was a hand-written manuscript,
copied later by scribes who devoted their lives to such tasks. Writing
under the name Fibonacci and borrowing from Persian manuscripts,
he strongly advocated the adoption of the Hindu-Arabic system of

numeration. He is credited by historians as having had enormous influence in the resulting changeover from Roman to Hindu-Arabic numerals. This was the principal message of *Liber Abaci* and its author's greatest contribution to Western civilization (see figure 8-3).

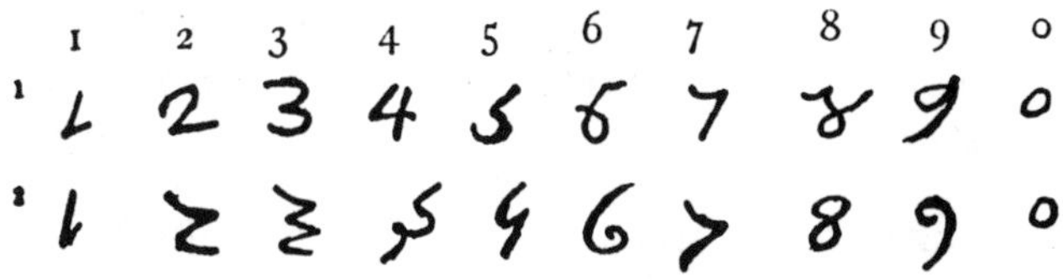

| 1 | 2 | 3 | 4 | 5 | 6 | 7 | 8 | 9 | 0 |

Figure 8-3

Hindu-Arabic numerals as Fibonacci recorded them in *Liber Abaci*. (Reprinted with permission from D. E. Smith, *History of Mathematics*, 71.)

Fibonacci wrote other books and revised *Liber Abaci* in 1228. His writings dealt with a wide range of topics, including abstract mathematics, algebra, geometry, and problem solving. He introduced the use of a line to separate the numbers in common fractions, although he wrote mixed numbers with the fraction to the left rather than to the right, as shown in figure 8-4. This style is believed to be related to the Arabic practice of right-to-left writing. He designed one of the earliest square root symbols (no longer in use today), shown in figure 8-5. He was one of the first mathematicians to give open-minded

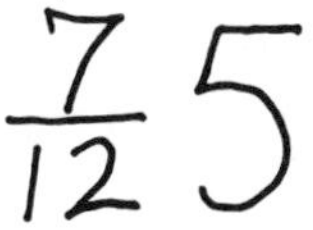

$$\frac{7}{12} \, 5$$

Figure 8-4

A mixed number as Leonardo wrote it.

Figure 8-5

Fibonacci's square root symbol.

consideration to the concept of negative numbers; when struggling with one financial problem, he suggested that it would be impossible to solve unless it were conceded that the problem began with a debt.

By the mid-1220s, Fibonacci's fame had drawn the attention of the Holy Roman emperor, Frederick II, a patron of science. Fibonacci was invited to appear before his court for a math tournament, which was somewhat like present-day math contests. Here is one of the problems:

> Find a rational number (whole number or common fraction) such that when 5 is added to its square or subtracted from its square, the result (in either case) is the square of another rational number.

Without the benefit of a calculator or computer, Fibonacci arrived at the correct answer: $41/12$!

$$(41/12)^2 + 5 = (49/12)^2$$
$$(41/12)^2 - 5 = (31/12)^2$$

Little is known about Fibonacci after 1240. He is believed to have died during that decade, but the Hindu-Arabic numerals he so enthusiastically promoted in Europe did not. Change came slowly, to be sure, and for a time the numerals were actually banned by merchants in some areas because of exploitation of those who were not familiar with them. But they spread rapidly throughout Europe during the Renaissance, especially after the invention of movable type for printing (1440), which led to new textbooks. Although there is evidence that the new numerals were used on some grave markers by the late 1200s, they really didn't take hold in Europe for about 300 years. Curiously, that is exactly how long it took for the Leaning Tower of Pisa to be built.

Following the publication of *Liber Abaci*, no significant mathematical works appeared until the beginning of the sixteenth century. Then, in 1509, with the help of no less an illustrator than Leonardo da Vinci, a monk named Luca Pacioli published *De Divina Proportione*—on the subject of the "divine proportion."

In 1611, German astronomer Johann Kepler arrived at the numbers illustrated by Fibonacci's rabbit sequence in his own work. There is no indication that he had access to any of Fibonacci's writings.

Kepler noted that "as 5 is to 8, so is 8 to 13, practically, and as 8 is to 13, so is 13 to 21 almost."*

During the next two centuries, many scholars investigated the sequence, deriving formulas and functions and solving problems. In about 1830, A. Braun first applied the sequence to the arrangement of bracts on a pinecone. A decade later, J. P. M. Binet derived a formula for finding the value of any Fibonacci number, given that its place in the sequence is known (see figure 8-6). In the mid-1800s, the revised version of *Liber Abaci* was formally published (printed). Soon thereafter, French mathematician Edouard Lucas named the sequence after Fibonacci, thereby distinguishing it from the one named after himself.

$$\text{The } n^{th} \text{ Fibonacci Number} = \frac{1}{\sqrt{5}}\left(\frac{1+\sqrt{5}}{2}\right)^n - \frac{1}{\sqrt{5}}\left(\frac{1-\sqrt{5}}{2}\right)^n$$

(For large n's, the second term can be neglected.)

Figure 8-6

Formula for finding the value of any Fibonacci number.

In about 1920, A. H. Church, an Oxford University botanist, discovered that the spirals on sunflower heads corresponded to the numbers in Fibonacci's rabbit problem. This discovery inspired botanists to look for Fibonacci numbers elsewhere. Much investigation followed, along with speculation on such matters as why phyllotactic ratios tend to be Fibonacci ratios, something that is not entirely resolved to this day.

Later that same decade, Professor Jay Hambidge of Yale University coined the name "dynamic symmetry" for proportions based on irrational numbers. This symmetry of growth is distinguished from static symmetry, in which areas are divided evenly into halves, thirds, and quarters. Dynamic symmetry is epitomized by the equiangular spiral of a shell and the beautiful off-center balance of a pinecone.

In the 1930s, Joseph Schillinger consciously composed music using Fibonacci intervals, and Ralph Elliot began predicting the stock market in Fibonacci periods.

---

*Maxey Brooke, "Fibonacci Numbers: Their History Through 1900," *Fibonacci Quarterly* 2 (April 1964): 149.

In the 1960s, in response to a lively interest aroused in Fibonacci numbers by that time, the Fibonacci Association was founded by mathematicians in California. The purpose of this organization is to exchange ideas and stimulate research on Fibonacci numbers and related topics. The association is alive and well today, headquartered at Santa Clara University in Santa Clara, California. It has published the *Fibonacci Quarterly* journal four times a year since 1962.

In 1984, the First International Conference on Fibonacci Numbers and Their Applications was held at the University of Patras, Greece. About 50 mathematicians from 13 countries gathered to exchange information and ideas on mathematical topics relating to Fibonacci numbers. In 1986, the Second International Conference took place at San Jose State University, San Jose, California, and the Third International Conference was expected to take place, appropriately, in Pisa, Italy.

The 1228 version of *Liber Abaci* can now be found at the Central National Library in Florence, Italy. It is the first volume of a two-volume work entitled *Scritti di Leonardo Pisano (The Writings of Leonardo Pisano)*, edited and published by Baldassare Boncompagni in about 1860.

Today a statue of Fibonacci stands in a garden in Pisa, across the Arno River from the Leaning Tower. In addition, two streets in Italy have been named for him—one in Pisa and one in Florence. These are simple tributes to a man who has been compared to his contemporary, St. Francis of Assisi; the latter brought light to the souls of men and women at the same time and in the same place that Fibonacci brought light to the science of mathematics. He would be delighted to see how brightly that light shines today.

Bibliography

Adams-Webber, J. "A Further Test of the Golden Section Hypothesis." *British Journal of Psychology* 69 (1978), 439–42.

Adler, Irving. *The Giant Golden Book of Mathematics.* New York: Golden Press, 1960.

Aieta, Joseph F. "Microworlds: Options for Learning and Teaching Geometry." *Mathematics Teacher,* September 1985.

Asimov, Isaac. *Asimov on Numbers.* New York: Doubleday & Co., 1977.

Basin, S. L. "The Fibonacci Sequence As It Appears in Nature." *Fibonacci Quarterly* 1 (February 1963): 53–64.

Beerbower, James R. *A Search for the Past.* Englewood Cliffs, NJ: Prentice-Hall, 1960.

Benjafield, J., and J. Adams-Webber. "The Golden Section Hypothesis." *British Journal of Psychology* 67, no. 1 (1976): 11–15.

Bergamini, David. *Mathematics.* Morristown, NJ: Silver Burdett General Learning Corp., 1970.

Brousseau, Br. U. Alfred. *An Introduction to Fibonacci Discovery.* San Jose, CA: San Jose State University, The Fibonacci Association, 1965.

———. "Fibonacci Statistics in Conifers." *Fibonacci Quarterly* 7 (December 1969): 525–32.

———. "On the Trail of the California Pine." *Fibonacci Quarterly* 6 (February 1968): 69–76.

Cajori, Florian. *A History of Mathematics.* New York: Macmillan Co., 1893.

Coates, Kevin. *Geometry, Proportion, and the Art of Lutherie.* Oxford: Clarendon Press, 1980.

Cook, Theodore Andrea. *The Curves of Life.* New York: Dover Publications, 1979.

Coxeter, H. S. M. *Introduction to Geometry.* New York: John Wiley & Sons, 1961.

Dalton, LeRoy C. *Algebra in the Real World.* Palo Alto, CA: Dale Seymour Publications, 1983.

Davis, T. Anthony, and Rudolf Altevogt. "Golden Mean of the Human Body." *Fibonacci Quarterly* 17 (December 1979): 340–44.

Deininger, Rolf. "Fibonacci Numbers and Water Pollution Control." *Fibonacci Quarterly* 10 (April 1972): 299–302.

Donald in Mathmagic Land. Glendale, CA: Walt Disney Educational Media, 1960. (Film)

Eves, Howard W. *In Mathematical Circles.* Boston: Prindle, Weber & Schmidt, 1969.

"The Fibonacci Numbers." *Time,* 4 April 1969.

Fibonacci Quarterly. Published by The Fibonacci Association, Santa Clara University, Santa Clara, CA, 1963–1986.

Fischer, Kurt. "The Fibonacci Sequence Encountered in Nerve Physiology." *Fibonacci Quarterly* 14 (November 1976): 377–79.

"Forbidden Fivefold Symmetry May Indicate Quasicrystal Phase." *Physics Today,* February 1985.

Gardner, Helen. *Art Through the Ages.* New York: Harcourt Brace Jovanovich, 1980.

Gardner, Martin. "A Discussion of Helical Structures, from Corkscrews to DNA Molecules." *Scientific American,* June 1963.

——— . *Mathematical Circus.* New York: Alfred A. Knopf, 1979.

——— . *Mathematics, Magic and Mystery.* New York: Dover Publications, 1956.

——— . "The Multiple Fascination of the Fibonacci Sequence." *Scientific American,* March 1969.

——— . *The 2nd Scientific American Book of Mathematical Puzzles and Diversions.* New York: Simon and Schuster, 1961.

Gettings, Fred. *The Meaning and Wonder of Art.* New York: Golden Press, 1963.

Ghyka, Matila. *The Geometry of Art and Life.* New York: Dover Publications, 1977.

Gies, Joseph and Frances. *Leonardo of Pisa and the New Mathematics of the Middle Ages.* New York: Thomas Y. Crowell, 1969.

Golden Section. Wilmette, IL: Films, Inc., Macmillan Films, 1968. (Film)

Hambidge, Jay. *The Elements of Dynamic Symmetry.* New York: Dover Publications, 1919.

Haughey, Bruce. *Dynamic Composition.* Billings, MT: Haughey Studios, 1983.

Hedian, Helene. "The Golden Section and the Artist." *Fibonacci Quarterly* 14 (December 1976): 406–18.

Hoffer, Alan. *Mathematics in Nature Posters.* Palo Alto, CA: Creative Publications, 1978.

Hoffer, William. "A Magic Ratio Occurs Throughout Art and Nature." *Smithsonian,* December 1975.

Hoggatt, Verner E. "Number Theory: The Fibonacci Sequence." In *1977 Yearbook of Science and the Future.* Chicago: Encyclopedia Britannica, 1976.

———. *Fibonacci and Lucas Numbers.* Boston: Houghton Mifflin, 1969.

Horadam, A. F. "Further Appearance of the Fibonacci Sequence." *Fibonacci Quarterly* 1 (December 1963): 41–46.

Huntley, E. H. *The Divine Proportion: A Study in Mathematical Beauty.* New York: Dover Publications, 1970.

Impressionism. Seacaucus, NJ: Chartweil Books, 1971.

Jacobs, Harold R. *Mathematics: A Human Endeavor.* San Francisco: W. H. Freeman, 1970.

Janson, H. W. *History of Art.* New York: Prentice-Hall and Harry Abrams, 1962.

Karchmar, E. J. "Phyllotaxis." *Fibonacci Quarterly* 3 (February 1965): 64–66.

Kenyon, Raymond G. *I Can Learn about Calculators and Computers.* New York: Harper & Brothers, 1961.

King, Charles. "Leonardo Fibonacci." *Fibonacci Quarterly* 1 (December 1963): 15–19.

Land, Frank. *The Language of Mathematics.* London: John Murray, 1960.

Larson, Paul. "The Golden Section in the Earliest Notated Western Music." *Fibonacci Quarterly* 9 (December 1978): 513-15.

Lowman, Edward A. "Some Striking Proportions in the Music of Béla Bartók." *Fibonacci Quarterly* 9 (December 1971): 527–37.

McNabb, Sister Mary de Sales. "Phyllotaxis." *Fibonacci Quarterly* 1 (December 1963): 57–60.

Meyer, Jerome. *Fun with Mathematics.* New York: World Publishing Co., 1952.

Monzingo, M. G. "Why Are 8:18 and 10:09 Such Pleasant Times?" *Fibonacci Quarterly* 21 (May 1983): 107–10.

Moore, Richard E. M. "Mosaic Units: Patterns in Ancient Mosaics." *Fibonacci Quarterly* 8 (April 1970): 281–310.

Newman, James. *The World of Mathematics,* 4 vols. New York: Simon and Schuster, 1956.

Norden, Hugo. "Proportions in Music." *Fibonacci Quarterly* 2 (October 1964): 219–22.

Prechter, Robert, and Alfred J. Frost. *Elliot Wave Principle.* Gainesville, GA: New Classics Library, 1978.

Ravielli, Anthony. *An Adventure in Geometry.* New York: Viking Press, 1957.

Read, B. A. "Fibonacci Series in the Solar System." *Fibonacci Quarterly* 8 (October 1970): 428–38.

Rhodes, F. H. T. *Fossils: A Guide to Prehistoric Life.* New York: Golden Press, 1962.

Runion, Garth E. *The Golden Section and Related Curiosa.* Glenview, IL: Scott Foresman & Co., 1972.

Schillinger, Joseph. *The Schillinger System of Musical Composition.* New York: Carl Fischer, 1941.

Sharp, W. E. "Fibonacci Drainage Patterns." *Fibonacci Quarterly* 10 (December 1972): 643–55.

Smith, D. E. *History of Mathematics.* New York: Dover Publications, 1923.

Stevens, Peter S. *Patterns in Nature.* Boston: Little, Brown & Co., 1974.

Terry, Sara. "Energy Studies Bring Rewards to Innovative High Schoolers." *The Christian Science Monitor,* 13 July 1982.

Thompson, D'Arcy W. *On Growth and Form.* Cambridge: Cambridge University Press, 1917.

Vorob'ev, N. N. *Fibonacci Numbers.* New York: Blaisdell, 1961.

Index